T0128898

MENTAL ILLNESS AMONG SOUTH ASIAN AMERICANS

MENTAL ILLNESS AMONG SOUTH ASIAN AMERICANS

Twenty Culturally Mindful Case Studies

Vani A. Rao, MD
Nalini V. Juthani, MD
Matthew E. Peters, MD

MENTAL ILLNESS AMONG SOUTH ASIAN AMERICANS
TWENTY CULTURALLY MINDFUL CASE STUDIES

Note to the Reader: This book is not meant to substitute for medical care of people and or South Asians with mental illness. The book should only be used as a guide to help facilitate interactive conversations between the individual and his or her clinicians.

iUniverse books may be ordered through booksellers or by contacting:

iUniverse
1663 Liberty Drive
Bloomington, IN 47403
www.iuniverse.com
1-800-Authors (1-800-288-4677)

ISBN: 978-1-5320-7347-2 (sc)
ISBN: 978-1-5320-7348-9 (e)

Library of Congress Control Number: 2019904371

Print information available on the last page.

iUniverse rev. date: 04/15/2019

Dedication

To our patients, who have taught us to be sensitive and to respect cultural diversity.

To the families of our patients who sacrifice immensely to help their loved ones and guide clinicians to understand their individual cultural values.

List of Contributors

Asha S Mishra MD

Diplomat ABPN in Adult and Geriatric Psychiatry
Distinguished Life Fellow of American Psychiatric Association
Clinical Professor of Psychiatry at VCU HS
Medical Director, Chesterfield CSB
Chair Board of Trustees, Indo-American Psychiatric Association

Bhagirathy Sahasranaman, MD
Distinguished Fellow, American Psychiatric Association
Distinguished Fellow, American Academy of Child and Adolescent
Psychiatry

Chetana Bhat MS, LCPC
Founder and CEO, Personal, Professional, Relationship Development
(PPRD)
Marriage Counselor trained in Imago Therapy and Guttmann's Method
(I & II)
Executive Coach, Workshop Presenter, and Public Speaker

Indrani Mookerjee, DSW, LCSW-C
IME Behavioral Health, LLC
Owner, IME Behavioral Health, LLC
Mental health expert advisor, Asian American Intercommunity Service (AICS)
Founding member, Counsellors Helping Asian Indians (CHAI)

Manan J. Shah, MD, FAPA
Child & Adolescent Psychiatrist,
Service Chief, Child & Adolescent Day Hospital
Sheppard Pratt Health System,
Towson, MD 21204

Manoj R. Shah, MD
Distinguished Life Fellow, American Psychiatric Association
Distinguished Life Fellow, American Academy of Child and Adolescent
Psychiatry
Founding Member, Past President, Past Chair of Board of Trustees, Indo-
American Psychiatric Association
Retired Associate Professor of Clinical Psychiatry, Donald and Barbara
School of Medicine at Hofstra-Northwell, NY

Matthew E. Peters, MD
Assistant Professor
Department of Psychiatry and Behavioral Sciences, Department of
Neurology
Johns Hopkins University School of Medicine

Nalini V. Juthani, MD
Retired, Professor of Psychiatry, Albert Einstein College of Medicine
Past Psychiatric Residency Training Director
Past Chair, Board of Trustees, and
President, Indo-American Psychiatric Association
Distinguished Life Fellow, American Psychiatric Association

Nurun N. Begum, MD, PhD
Consultant Psychiatrist
Delaware Psychiatric Center, Newcastle, DE
Rockford Center, Universal Health Services (UHS), Newark, DE

Rachna Raisinghani, MD, FAPA,
Adult and Consultation-Liaison Psychiatry,
Sheppard Pratt Health System,
Towson, MD 21204

Ramaswamy Viswanathan, MD, DMSc, DLFAPA
Professor, Department of Psychiatry and Behavioral Sciences
State University of New York Downstate Medical Center, Brooklyn, NY
Past Chair, Board of Trustees, and Past President, Indo-American
Psychiatric Association
Board of Trustees, American Psychiatric Association, 2017-2019

Razia F. Kosi, LCSW-C, Doctoral Candidate, Johns Hopkins University
Founder, Former Executive Director, Counselors Helping (South)
Asians, Inc.
Facilitator, Office of Diversity, Equity, and Inclusion, Howard County
Public Schools.
Therapist, Consultant.

Rohit M. Chandra MD.
Child and Adolescent Psychiatrist, Massachusetts General Hospital
Instructor in Psychiatry, Harvard Medical School

Sailaja Menon MS, CAGS
Ex Faculty Associate, Dept. of Counseling, Johns Hopkins University.
Licensed Counseling Psychologist
Lifeworks Holistic Counseling Centre
Dubai

Sandeep Vaishnavi, MD, PhD
Neuropsychiatrist, Duke University Medical Center
Director, Clinical Trials and Transcranial Magnetic Stimulation, Carolina
Partners

Contents

Foreword

Psychiatric illnesses are relatively common and extremely debilitating. They are one of the top causes of disability worldwide, and in the United States many patients with very treatable illnesses such as depression and anxiety do not seek care due to issues related to misinformation and stigma about these illnesses. As a result there is a significant number of individuals who unnecessarily suffer because they do not believe they have treatable medical illnesses. This series of case studies is a tremendous contribution as it brings to life many of the critical issues faced by those with psychiatric illness and underscores the variable presentations influenced by cultural issues. Having this information available to educate individuals with these illnesses, their families and their treatment providers about subtle differences in presentation highly influenced by cultural issues is invaluable. Unfortunately, many cultural groups in the United States are not open to treatment of psychiatric illness. To make progress in reaching those who need help, providers need to combine making culturally specific arguments that are respectful of the competing ideas individuals have about their psychiatric symptoms while being clear about the potential benefit of treatment. Through these illustrative cases, South Asian mental health professionals, including psychiatrists, therapists, and counselors, outline for the reader common issues that arise during treatment and provide insight into culturally sensitive ways to address the issues and achieve successful treatment. Being able to read cases in which South Asian individuals have psychiatric illnesses recognized and successfully treated, will hopefully motivate many individuals to be more open to treatment.

As a non-South Asian psychiatrist, I found this series of cases extremely helpful. Thinking about the differences in how individuals experience psychiatric illness and react to having these illness underscores the importance of spending the time needed to really get to know your patients. It is also very important to not fall into the trap of believing there will be many similarities among a group of patients with a shared culture. The challenge and reward of treating patients from diverse cultures is needing to spend adequate time to understand each person's life experiences – within a culture, a family and an individual life.

The following twenty case histories are presented in ways which convey a depth of understanding not only of mental illness but of the underlying cultural beliefs and values and the challenges encountered within families when traditional beliefs and practices are not embraced. The authors are sensitive to inter-generational biases and convey a sensitivity to not only the struggles faced by first generation immigrants but those of subsequent generations. Artfully, while providing histories, diagnostic formulations, management strategies and teaching points, there are discussions of how cultural belief systems can be integrated within conventional treatment. This is always done through a lens of respecting culture and convey nuanced insights into perceptions both of patients and their families.

Each case outlines important take away learning points and cultural issues to consider in treatment. Teaching points conveyed by the authors always contain pearls of wisdom as shown in the case of Ravi below.

"Establishing rapport and forming a therapeutic relationship is a critical first step in treatment. It becomes particularly important when cultural and religious sensitivities are in play. Being knowledgeable is always an advantage, but in the absence of knowledge, being open to learning with a non-judgmental stance is helpful."

Other cases help us to understand the complexity of being treated with in a close community and the issues of confidentiality that may arise as well as the particular family dynamics that many South Asian multigenerational families have. A theme throughout the cases is the critical need for culturally sensitive and respectful education of those with the illness and their families. Given the close connection that many South Asian families maintain, successful treatment requires the investment of time to educate the family members supporting the patient. As well, the opportunity to build a therapeutic alliance based on a potential cultural bias supporting trusting an authority figure such as a physician is also discussed.

There is always more to learn.

Through my own experience of over 20 years focusing on the treatment of depression and bipolar disorder, I have seen how common it is for individuals to focus on the details of their life and explain away symptoms rather than looking for the clinical symptoms that confirm that they have a treatable illness. Throughout these cases I was struck by the risk of cultural differences being used as a way to have an alternative explanation rather than the truth of a serious medical issue. It is challenging and often unwelcome to receive a psychiatric diagnosis, and many individuals would like any other explanation instead. As a psychiatrist who hopes to be sensitive to cultural issues, there is a trap of being so focused on these differences that one could miss the underlying clinical symptoms. These cases beautifully demonstrate common presentations of psychiatric illnesses in South Asian patients and the types of variation in symptoms that might be commonly seen among this group.

Finally, I want to express my admiration and gratitude for the South Asian psychiatrists, therapists, and counselors who have demonstrated devotion to their community with the creation of this case series. Without question their service to patients in the South Asian community is invaluable. By investing the effort to share their experiences, a broader range of individuals with these illnesses and their families can be educated as can non-South Asian mental health providers. In reading these cases, I was struck by how many subtle yet critical cultural issues I may be missing. I am indebted to have the opportunity to improve my own knowledge and know that many others will similarly benefit. This is a wonderful addition to the psychiatric literature and a tremendous resource for patients, families, and providers.

Karen L. Swartz, M.D.
Myra S. Meyer Associate Professor in Mood Disorders
Vice Chair for Faculty, Department of Psychiatry and Behavioral Sciences
Director of Clinical and Educational Programs, The Johns Hopkins Mood Disorders Center
Director, Adolescent Depression Awareness Program (ADAP)
The Johns Hopkins Hospital/Meyer 3-181
Baltimore, MD 21287-7381

Acknowledgement

The idea of writing this book was born a few years ago when the editors and Dr. Asha Mishra conducted an informal survey and discussions to determine do's and don'ts in the evaluation and management of persons of South Asian origin living in the United States. Results revealed knowledge of the culture as an important factor in effectively working with persons of South Asian origin. Based on this information, we have put together twenty case reports.

We are grateful to Dr. Asha Mishra for her input and for motivating us to bring this book to fruition.

We are extremely grateful to all our authors for their contribution. We offer a big thank you to each of the authors.

The publishers, Dr. Vani Rao, and Dr. Nalini Juthani have deeply enjoyed working with the third editor, Dr. Mathew Peters, whose contributions have made this book richer.

We are gratified that we are able to give back our knowledge and skills to psychiatric and non-psychiatric clinicians who help South Asian patients and their families.

Last but not the least, we are grateful to our spouses and families whose support has encouraged us to bring this book to fruition.

Vani Rao, Nalini Juthani & Mathew Peters.

Introduction

The Asian American community more broadly is a heterogeneous population differing in language, religion, and cultural values. We have chosen to focus specifically on South Asian Americans because this book is based on the years of experience of South Asian clinicians practicing in the U.S. Each case study offers a unique approach to address cultural beliefs and values that may facilitate or hinder that individual's interactions and coping with emotional distress.

Over the last decade, there has been a steep growth in the South Asian population in the United States—individuals immigrating from India, Pakistan, Nepal, Sri Lanka, Bhutan, and Bangladesh. While some of these immigrants are able to transition easily and adapt to the Western culture, others encounter various challenges. These challenges are not only acculturation-related, but also involve difficulty in obtaining gainful employment and medical care. With regards to the latter, while South Asians may find it easier to approach their physicians regarding physical health problems, it is more challenging when it comes to mental health issues. The main reasons for not seeking mental health treatment include: (1) stigma associated with diagnosis of mental illness, which often is perceived as 'mental weakness' or a 'character flaw;' (2) cultural beliefs and values - e.g., suffering is part of life, suffering is punishment for sins committed in previous births; (3) concerns about not being understood by treating physicians – e.g., non-South Asian physicians may not understand their background and cultural values and hence may not be able to provide appropriate treatment; (4) concerns regarding confidentiality - physicians may either be known to the patient personally or to someone in the community and confidentiality may be compromised. Other miscellaneous reasons include the shame and embarrassment associated with carrying a diagnosis of mental illness, lack of insurance, language barriers, disinterest in psychotherapy, and concerns about long-term treatment with medications.

In addition to patient-related issues, there are also reports that clinicians find mental health assessment and treatment of South Asian Americans challenging because of (1) a lack of research studies on South Asian American mental illness and hence poor understanding of culturally-sensitive phenomenology and treatment, (2) clinical variation in presentation of symptoms due to tendency to focus on somatic symptoms, and (3) minimal knowledge of the heterogeneous South Asian American culture and values. Clinicians may also view South Asian patients as 'time consuming' as they tend to come with several family members who would each like to have time, as a group and individually, with the clinician. While some strides are being made to educate South Asian Americans on mental health issues via workshops and conferences, it is also important to educate clinicians to be culturally proficient so that they can be more responsive to the mental health needs of South Asian Americans.

It is with this background that we have compiled a series of case studies on a range of mental illness presentations among South Asian Americans treated by senior South Asian clinicians (e.g., psychiatrists, therapists, counselors) practicing in the U.S. As some of the patients were treated by the clinician authors several years ago, the diagnosis assigned is not always based on the current *Diagnostic and Statistical Manual 5* (*DSM5*) criteria nor was a Cultural Formulation Interview (CFI) used in the evaluation and management. Also, as the predominant goal of the book is to highlight South Asian American cultural aspects in presentation and management, we have allowed each author to highlight cultural factors pertinent to that case.

To maintain confidentiality and protect the privacy of patients and their families, the authors have modified the identities of patients while carefully maintaining the essential cultural aspects and teaching points of the case. For the same reasons, we have also chosen not to mention the name of the authors responsible for each case report, but have instead included their names (alphabetical order by last name) in the Acknowledgement section. Collectively, the authors have treated many diverse South Asian American patients over the last several years. They are clinicians and educators who have added great value to this book by identifying teaching points. The cases are presented in a loosely formulaic manner (e.g., same headings), but otherwise are presented in the manner of each individual author's training and background. We are sincerely grateful and whole-heartedly acknowledge their contribution. Dr. Matthew Peters is our non-South Asian editor and educator, who has made sure that the cultural issues identified in this book are clearly understood by clinicians who may not be as well-versed with cultural issues as the South Asian clinician authors may be. Dr. Peters' edits have added special value to this book.

We hope that this book will serve as a guide to inform clinicians about some cultural values of South Asian Americans and the influence of these cultural values on the presentation and treatment of emotional distress. This book is not about multiculturalism or about cultural competency. It is well-known that attaining the latter takes years of training and working for long periods with a specific ethnic population. The formulation, treatment, and teaching points discussed for each case applies to that specific case. While some of the principles can be extrapolated to other similar cases, clinicians should be aware of individual differences and circumstances unique to each individual.

Ankur: Untreated Attention Deficit Disorder and Cultural Isolation

Case History

Ankur, a 26-year-old single male graduate student of Asian-Indian descent, was asked to take a medical leave of absence in the setting of two behavioral outbursts in the academic setting. He presented for psychiatric evaluation and clearance to return to his studies.

Ankur was born in the United States of first generation immigrant parents. Both parents were healthcare professionals. Ankur's mother had good prenatal care and his delivery was uncomplicated. His development milestones were normal outside of mild difficulties with articulation, which were persistent. He was the second of two siblings. His older sister was healthy and performed well academically. He had a good relationship with her.

Ankur began school without any separation issues and adjusted well. He had a hard time making friends due to limited social skills, but he did not have any behavioral problems. Ankur's parents socialized with fellow Indian immigrants and Ankur again did not engage with other children but was content to play by himself. He was a bright student, did well in his studies, but was socially awkward. He went through high school without much difficulty as he was a hard working student and his parents encouraged academics above other activities. He did not take part in sports, music, or drama. At times, he was teased and bullied for being a nerd, but he kept his emotions to himself and immersed himself in studies as his parents expected. The school did not intervene as there were no complaints and he did not have behavioral issues. In college, he began to have difficulties with focus and getting his work done on time. Despite this, he worked hard, graduated, and was accepted into graduate school. The workload in the graduate school was heavy; he began falling behind and experienced an increased level of stress. He did not smoke, drink or use any drugs.

Because of his academic difficulties, he underwent a neuropsychological and psychiatric assessment. Neuropsychological testing revealed an average range of intelligence, and the cognitive profile suggested Attention Deficit Disorder, Inattentive Type. He displayed weaknesses in organizational and metalinguistic skills (abstract thinking). Psychiatric evaluation revealed low self-esteem, lack of confidence, and comorbid major depression. Psychotherapy, extended time for exams, academic tutoring, and possible medication for attention difficulties were recommended. He was placed on a stimulant by a neurologist to help improve his attention span. However, there was no follow-up for his psychiatric issues.

Ankur continued to do poorly in school. He struggled to keep up his grades and complete his assignments on time. In addition, he developed significant anxiety in the setting of his academic struggles and felt that he had brought shame to his family. His parents did express disapproval of his academic struggles. Two incidents later occurred that forced him to go on medical leave of absence. First, he had a minor verbal altercation with one of the cafeteria staff due to the staff member having difficulty understanding Ankur. Second, he had an explosive outburst with his roommates as they were playing loud music and paid no heed to his multiple requests of turning the volume down. The roommates reported Ankur to the authorities for using foul language and threatening to kill them. The school authorities suggested that he take a leave of absence for psychiatric evaluation and treatment.

Immediately after the cafeteria episode, Ankur was seen by a Caucasian psychiatrist through the college healthcare center. Though a formal diagnosis of psychotic episode was not made, a neuroleptic medication was prescribed. Ankur developed joint pains and stiffness of muscles and the medication was discontinued. He then chose to see a private South Asian-Indian psychiatrist. At the time of initial evaluation with the psychiatrist, a detailed history including birth, development, early childhood history, and psychosocial history was obtained. Cultural issues were assessed by meeting with the parents and the sister separately. Neuropsychological test results and school report cards were reviewed. With Ankur's permission, the Dean of the college was also contacted for collateral history.

At the time of the initial evaluation, Ankur appeared distraught, embarrassed, and angry. He had not been taking the prescribed stimulant, as he did not find it helpful. He acknowledged making threats to his roommates, but denied intent to hurt or harm. He explained that the statements were made in the heat of the moment, as he was stressed about upcoming exams. He denied symptoms of major depression, mania, hypomania, psychosis, generalized anxiety disorder, or panic attacks. He reported feeling stressed about his poor academic performance and bringing shame to his family. He seemed motivated to return to college and complete his studies.

Mental status examination at the time of the initial evaluation revealed Ankur to be a young male in his mid-20s of Asian-Indian descent. He was casually dressed, cooperative, related well, and maintained good eye contact. He was not guarded or evasive. His mood was anxious and tense. He was worried about his future and frustrated that he had to take a year off when he did not really mean to hurt anyone. He did show some dysfluency in speech, but his thought process was logical, relevant, and coherent. He gave his version of events rather succinctly. No thought disorder, paranoia, or ideas of reference were elicited. No perceptual disturbances were elicited (e.g., auditory or visual hallucinations). He endorsed sadness related to his situation and denied global feelings of depression. He denied active or passive suicidal or homicidal thoughts, intent, or plan. He was oriented to time, person, and place. He had no short- or long-term memory problems. He was aware that he had difficulties with organization and focusing which led to difficulties with studying.

Diagnostic Formulation

Ankur had difficulties with attention, organization, articulation, and social interactions since early childhood. He was teased and bullied in school. Despite these issues, he had no behavioral problems and did well academically, so no psychiatric intervention was done. His parents did not notice his social awkwardness or his isolation. They also did not seek any help for his articulation difficulties. They were content as he performed well in school and had no behavior problems. Ankur did not confide in his parents about the teasing in school. He kept his emotions to himself and immersed himself in studies to get their approval. During therapy, his frustrations with his parents became evident. He felt that his parents were highly critical and focused predominantly on his shortcomings and failures.

After the initial evaluation, the psychiatrist also met with his parents and sister regularly. His parents were mainly concerned about the medical leave of absence and the local Indian community finding out about it. They wanted the "issue" to be resolved as soon as possible so that Ankur could restart college and earn his degree. They also wanted him to keep up with schoolwork at home so that he could be ahead of his peers when he returned to school. They were embarrassed about his outbursts and furious at him for bringing shame to the family. On the positive side, they were ready to commit to have him come regularly for therapy sessions, try medications as recommended, and pay fees incurred. His sister confirmed Ankur's history, also felt that Ankur was overly sensitive, and did not handle criticism well. After considering all pertinent findings, diagnoses of Attention Deficit Disorder, Inattentive type and Adjustment Disorder with Mixed Anxiety and Depressed Mood were considered for management.

Management

Ankur was a cooperative patient who was motivated to restart school and complete his coursework. He and his parents realized that the school authorities were concerned about his outbursts and that psychiatric clearance was required before he could be reinstated. They readily gave permission to the psychiatrist to communicate with the Dean of the college.

The rationale for psychotropics including indications, risks, and benefits were explained by the psychiatrist to Ankur and his family. Ankur's parents encouraged him to take medications as prescribed and stay compliant with treatment. Ankur was placed on a different stimulant and the dose was gradually adjusted to clinically therapeutic levels. He was asked to get a planner, which helped him organize himself. This planner was to be used later when he went back to college so that he can plan his academic work and prepare for tests. He was also placed on an antidepressant to help with anxiety and mild depressive symptoms.

He was seen for individual therapy, where his sense of embarrassment and shame at letting his parents down were addressed. Working on his self-esteem was a major undertaking in individual therapy, which was eclectic in nature. Cognitive behavior therapy was helpful to improve his self-esteem whenever he went into a negative spiral.

It was stressed that he was a good person, had not committed any crimes, and did not have to be afraid or intimidated by authority figures. This message was repeated in follow-up sessions and he was told to focus on his achievements whenever negative feelings surfaced.

At first, it was challenging to work with Ankur's parents as they expected the psychiatrist and medications to treat all his issues. The psychiatrist spent a few sessions educating them about the role of a psychiatrist as a guide to help Ankur find solutions rather than present solutions. Ankur's parents were also concerned about the local Indian community learning of their son's psychiatric treatment and the shame this may bring to the family. The parents were assured that when they or Ankur came for an appointment, no other Indian family would be in the waiting area. If they ran into the treating provider at a social event, the plan was to acknowledge each other casually and never discuss Ankur. It was also made clear to the parents that Ankur's communication would be confidential and would not be divulged to them, except if there was any danger to life. Ankur felt reassured that he could discuss his feelings without fear of his parents or anyone else finding out.

The psychiatrist worked with both Ankur and his parents on the need and importance for maintaining both academic and non-academic activities. Ankur was encouraged to get a job at a local mall to keep his days structured. This also helped with his social isolation and exposure to a different culture. His parents' concerns about their son losing focus on his studies if he socialized and got distracted by engaging in extracurricular activities were discussed. It was explained that being aware of what is happening in the areas of sports, arts, or politics could help him socially.

They were advised that this would help him become part of a group and his self-esteem would improve. Ankur was encouraged to have some time to relax from his studies and watch sports, news, and go to a movie with his co-workers. He was reassured that his parents would not be critical of him or be angry with him if he did not study continuously.

His parents were also educated about the educational system, and the necessary steps that had to be taken to get Ankur reinstated. The Dean was kept in the loop about Ankur's progress. At the end of the leave of absence, the psychiatrist provided a letter indicating that Ankur had been compliant with psychiatric treatment and was in stable mental health. The psychiatrist also prepared Ankur for his interviews with the school authorities by conducting mock interviews. Ankur rejoined college and successfully graduated with a master's degree. At the time of this writing, he is gainfully employed and still attends follow-up sessions with his psychiatrist. Acculturation issues are still being addressed in ongoing therapy.

Summary

Ankur is a 26-year-old single male graduate student of Asian-Indian descent who was asked to take a leave of absence from his graduate school and get a psychiatric clearance before he could be reinstated. A careful evaluation of the episodes that led to the decision by the college, including getting first-hand information from the Dean (who would be instrumental in the decision to reinstate) was completed. A detailed history of Ankur's life was obtained from various sources including review of his school report cards. Neuropsychological evaluation report was very helpful in understanding Ankur's cognitive skills and limitations. The accurate diagnoses including psychosocial and cultural issues helped in planning therapeutic management and use of appropriate medication. Ultimately, Ankur was treated for Attention Deficit Disorder and Adjustment Disorder with Mixed Anxiety and Depressed Mood. At first, Ankur's parents were eager to get him reinstated in school and avoid embarrassment in their community. However, regular sessions with the psychiatrist gradually helped them understand Ankur's cognitive and emotional struggles. In addition, the importance of helping Ankur balance academic and non-academic activities, and alleviating the parent's fear of personal information leaking out to the community, was helpful. Ankur himself was motivated. He was bright and followed concrete directions well. Finally, periodic contact with the Dean to understand the requirements of the college was very helpful.

Teaching Points

1. Guaranteeing confidentiality to immigrants from the Asian-Indian community is essential. Many fear that information about them or their loved ones' psychiatric treatment can leak out to others in the community and therefore choose not to seek help from mental health professionals.

2. First generation immigrants value educational achievements at the expense of other non-academic skills, such as sports, arts, etc. At times, they can be parochial and not expose their children to other cultures for fear of losing values of their motherland. Children/ young adults often feel pressured to do extremely well in school and not participate in non-academic activities, which can lead to poor socialization and acculturation difficulties, in turn leading to lack of confidence and self-esteem. The clinician may need to emphasize the importance of balancing academic and non-academic skills to improve socialization and self-esteem.

Nina: Rapport Building, Family Dynamics, and Unrecognized Depression

Case History

Nina, a 21-year-old single female of Indian origin, presented to a community mental health clinic for management of the following symptoms: trouble focusing on her coursework, social isolation, poor time management, and poor grades. She presented to the office alone, however, prior to the initial appointment, Nina's father had numerous informal discussions with the clinic's psychiatrist about Nina's struggles. After much encouragement from the psychiatrist, Nina's father agreed to have her come for an evaluation.

A few years prior, Nina had undergone a comprehensive battery of cognitive tests and was diagnosed with Attention Deficit Hyperactivity Disorder (ADHD). At time of initial clinic evaluation, she denied symptoms concerning for major depressive or (hypo)manic episodes, anxiety, psychosis, or other emotional symptoms. In Nina's view, she only needed medication for ADHD. Given her subjective symptoms of inattention and difficulty focusing, and test results consistent with ADHD, she was started on a stimulant. Nina was compliant with treatment. She presented regularly for follow-up visits, but engaged minimally. She would always ask the psychiatrist if her treatment was being discussed with her parents, despite the psychiatrist assuring her that no information would be divulged to anyone without her written informed consent.

Gradually, as she developed a therapeutic relationship with her psychiatrist, she began to discuss other problems and symptoms. Her parents had immigrated from India prior to her birth. Both parents were physicians in private practice. She was the younger of two siblings. She described her childhood as "sheltered." Her relationship with her parents was affectionate, but she perceived her parents as strict and overprotective. Her older brother had just graduated from medical school and had matched into a residency program. Nina struggled with many subjects in school, but always did very well in math. After graduation from high school, she joined a local college, majoring in actuarial science.

Her parents were not happy with her choice of college major. Since it was the "family vocation", her parents wanted Nina to take pre-medicine courses. To please them, she did take a few of these courses, but did not do well and eventually went back to her chosen major. In addition, and much against her wish, she lived at home with her parents during college. In Nina's view, this was due to their overprotective nature. Her parents constantly compared her academic performance to her older brother who had done extremely well throughout his schooling. Nina would spend 8-10 hours a day studying at home and often declined opportunities to socialize with her friends. Despite this, her test scores did not match her effort and were much below her parents' expectations. Nina often felt lonely, sad, and anxious at home and chose to spend more time with her grandparents (who lived in the same household) instead of her parents. Her grandfather taught her to chant *Vedic mantras* from Hindu religion scriptures which helped alleviate her sadness and anxiety.

Another major stressor was related to dating. She was dating a young Caucasian male, but ended the relationship as soon as her parents became aware. Her parents were very upset and persuaded her to end the relationship because they had always hoped she would marry a boy from a similar ethnic and cultural background. Shortly thereafter, her parents began to search for a potential groom of Indian origin.

Nina's emotional health continued to decline. She began experiencing symptoms of persistent sadness, anhedonia, poor motivation, hopelessness, social isolation, and passive suicidal thoughts. She coped with her emotional symptoms by accepting it as fate or '*karma*'. She did not have any significant medical issues. Her menstrual cycles were regular, with no previous pregnancies. She rarely drank alcohol in social situations and did not smoke cigarettes, cannabis, or use other recreational drugs. There was no known history of any psychiatric disorders in the family. Her father was diagnosed with hypertension.

Diagnostic Formulation

Nina was diagnosed with ADHD based on subjective complaints of inattention and distractibility, as well as the results of cognitive testing. She also endorsed several core symptoms of major depressive disorder. Her symptoms of major depression were precipitated and maintained by several chronic and acute stressors.

There are several cultural factors that influenced Nina's presentation and each was considered in the diagnostic formulation. Nina's parents were part of a "model minority community." Like many immigrants from South Asia, they were highly educated professionals, who sought to impart the same values they were raised on (e.g., academic achievement above well-roundedness) to their children. That pressure to excel, along with the constant comparison to her brother, significantly impacted Nina's self-esteem. In addition, like many parents of South Asian origin, Nina's parents were overprotective, even into young adulthood. This influenced her choice of college based on proximity to home. Unlike her peers, Nina was not allowed to live at her college dormitory, which limited her social interactions. Nina's dating life was also a significant element of this case. Despite her boyfriend being a good student and a strong source of support for her, her parents' disapproved of the relationship as he was Caucasian. Nina's parents, like many Indian parents, wanted her to only date and ultimately marry an Indian man. This contributed to her frustration and sense of loss of control.

Lastly, a common cultural belief among Asians, especially Hindus, is the concept of '*karma*', which posits that an individual's present circumstances are a consequence of past choices and actions. While this may have helped Nina to cope with her illness to a certain extent, it propagated a sense of helplessness. It also contributed to a tendency to view her condition as untreatable and reluctance in seeking treatment.

Management

Most young adults presenting for psychiatric treatment present alone or with their parents or other family members. In this case, Nina's father took the initiative to contact the psychiatrist and remained deeply involved throughout her treatment. It is not uncommon in a South Asian context for parents of even an adult to seek help for their son/daughter. In South Asian culture, there may be delayed differentiation from the family and the adult may continue to live with his/her parents well into adulthood, regardless of financial independence. Due to this, the family often remains closely involved in medical treatment, creating a situation where constant family support may also lend to interference in treatment and a disruption in feelings of confidentiality. As seen in this case, Indian and other South Asian families are often joint, and extended family members may live under the same roof. This adds a further layer of family dynamics for each individual. It helps to be aware of this when treating individuals from a South Asian background.

Once Nina established care, the first challenge was to encourage her to take ownership of her health and be an active participant in her treatment. After building rapport, Nina was counseled about taking her parents into confidence and expressing her emotional issues and supportive needs to them. This required several family sessions in which both parents participated. The physician served as a mediator, helping Nina understand her parents' perspective about their expectations stemming from their traditional values and background. Her parents were educated about inter-generational biases that were creating a disconnect between Nina and them. Medication management was offered, to which Nina agreed, but her parents were skeptical. Family sessions assisted with gaining support from all parties and she was treated effectively with a stimulant for ADHD and an antidepressant for Major Depressive Disorder.

In family sessions, Nina's parents described their expectations from her. South Asian immigrants commonly have high expectations from their children, as they have usually faced numerous struggles (e.g., legal aspects of the immigration process, financial struggles, racial discrimination). This is especially true for first generation South Asians who are raised in a developing nation with fewer resources and immigrate to the West. It often takes several years to establish themselves and assimilate successfully into the American culture. Second generation South Asians tend to not have similar types of struggles. Hence, there is often a sense in the parents that their children are not working as hard and things have come easy to them without realizing the unique struggles of each generation. It is helpful for a mental health clinician to be aware of such inter-generational biases and address them appropriately in individual and family therapy.

Nina's romantic relationship was discussed in therapy. Arranged marriages within the community are a common feature of traditional South Asian values and is usually preferred over romantic marriages. When immigration is factored in, this preference tends to become stronger for many families as they are seen as an assured way of transmitting the community's values and culture to the younger generation. There may exist a fear of complete assimilation within the host culture as it may be thought to dilute traditional values. Hence, such families may put a lot more pressure on relationships even though having a relationship is a normal part of adolescent development. This is another potential cause of major inter-generational conflict in families of South Asian descent.

Taking into account cultural belief systems and incorporating this into conventional treatment is an essential component of treatment and significantly increases chances of response. As in this case, rather than meditation or mindfulness, the patient did a lot better when encouraged to continue practicing chanting *Vedic mantras* as it was already part of her belief system. Similarly, Yoga practices may be a very useful treatment tool as there may already be a degree of familiarity with these and similar practices. Another treatment consideration is autonomy. Whereas patient autonomy is key in Western medicine, the physician-patient relationship in most South Asian countries tends to take on a paternalistic role. Patients view physicians as authoritative and tend to not question physicians and may accept treatment suggestions unconditionally. Hence, it is possible that even if the patient has questions, they will be reluctant to ask them. Therefore, it is essential to encourage these patients to ask questions and engage them in a thorough risk versus benefit discussion to choose an appropriate course of treatment.

Summary

Nina is a 21-year-old single female of Indian origin who presented for treatment of ADHD, but ultimately received treatment for Major

Depressive Disorder and difficult family dynamics as well. The depressive symptoms were not initially expressed by patient or family and required building of rapport before the patient felt comfortable discussing them. The strain in her relationship with her parents was a major stressor. Given the significant impact of cultural issues in this case, it was important to understand these factors first and foremost and treat underlying mental illness in this context.

Teaching Points

1. It is important to be mindful of complex and intertwined family dynamics, and relatively delayed separation-individuation, when treating a young person of South Asian origin.
2. Emphasis on academics by South Asians may lead to a clinical presentation focused on cognitive disorders of mental life (e.g., inattention and ADHD) and clinicians must diligently build rapport and do a complete psychiatric review of symptoms to identify other comorbid conditions (e.g. Major Depressive Disorder).
3. South Asian culture is quite patriarchal and the burden of adjusting and adaptation often rests on women causing them additional emotional turmoil.
4. Marrying within the community is seen as a way of preserving cultural values and hence interracial marriages are often discouraged.
5. Patients of South Asian origin may at times find comfort in traditional practices and beliefs, even if not evidence-based in Western medicine.

Aparajita: Panic Disorder with Agoraphobia in a Stay-at-Home Mother

Case History

Aparajita, a 55-year-old married female of South Asian descent, is a stay-at-home mother of two who first sought psychiatric treatment at the age of 35. This case history describes treatment over the course of 20 years with the same psychiatrist.

Aparajita was born and raised in India. Birth, early development, and childhood history were unremarkable. She was a bright student, did well throughout her education, and obtained a master's degree. She got married in her late 20s and became pregnant soon after her marriage. During the second trimester of her pregnancy, she and her husband decided to travel to the United States (U.S.) to visit their extended family. She went into premature labor while waiting at the gate to board the international flight. She was taken to a local hospital and her daughter was born. Due to prematurity, her daughter was born with deafness and blindness.

Hoping to obtain better medical care for their daughter, Aparajita and her husband continued with their travel plans to the U.S. a few months later. They arrived in the U.S. without careful consideration of the finances and support they would need in raising a child with multiple handicaps. Shortly thereafter, Aparajita was diagnosed with hyperthyroidism and needed to undergo radiation treatment. The treatment left her with hypothyroidism, for which she had to take levothyroxine. Taking care of her daughter became Aparajita's priority and she taught herself braille. About four years later, the couple had a son, who was born full term, healthy, and attained developmental milestones within the normal range.

Aparajita spent all her time raising her children. She had no hobbies and no social activities.

A few years after the birth of her daughter, Aparajita began to have panic attacks, which gradually increased in frequency and intensity. She experienced these attacks as a spontaneous, sudden feeling of edginess associated with physical symptoms of chest discomfort, dizziness, unsteadiness, tremors, sweating, choking sensation, and queasiness in her stomach. At first, she ignored the attacks, believing that suffering was common and had to be endured silently. Later, as the attacks increased, the physical symptoms of chest and stomach discomfort became more bothersome and she made several visits to the emergency department (ED) and her primary care provider (PCP). It is unclear what diagnosis or treatment was offered, but there was no improvement in her symptoms.

Aparajita gradually developed an intense fear of leaving her home and finally decided to seek psychiatric treatment. The home boundedness interfered with her ability to take care of her family. During the initial psychiatric evaluation, she endorsed additional symptoms of apprehension about the future, fear of death, and worries that her children would not be properly cared for. She did not report any symptoms of depression. She endorsed a struggle balancing care of her deaf/blind daughter and her "normal" son. She worried about loving one more at the expense of the other and verbalized feelings of guilt. She also shared ambivalent feelings about living in the U.S. as she missed the support and closeness with her family of origin. She had not visited India in over seven years at time of initial evaluation. She missed her "life of freedom in India" and felt life in the U.S. was full of restrictions, despite being in a good marriage with support from her husband and extended family. She was on a therapeutic dose of levothyroxine and was not on any other medications. She was in good physical health otherwise and had no history of substance use. There was no family history of mental illness. Payment for continued psychiatric treatment was another stressor as her husband was self-employed and they were uninsured. Attending a state-funded clinic was her only option.

She was diagnosed as having Panic Disorder with Agoraphobia and was started on a short-acting benzodiazepine to be taken as needed. She was not interested in talk therapy and preferred to be seen only by the psychiatrist for medication management. During the medication management sessions, the psychiatrist used extra time to discuss Aparajita's feelings and help her cope with her struggles and ambivalence. At first, Aparajita remained passive in treatment and preferred the psychiatrist to take the lead and direct her. The provided psychotherapy focused on finding solutions for common life problems. Later, Aparajita became more comfortable with discussing her stressors and even requested information on resources for her daughter. Over the course of treatment, she stabilized and reported improvement in her symptoms. She came to accept as normal her "guilt" about loving one child more than the other child. She was very open to self-reflection and readily completed assigned tasks, including making time for self-care. Her daughter also progressively obtained more services, such as disability insurance and rehabilitation. Over time, Aparajita's medication was switched to a long-acting benzodiazepine.

Aparajita's visits to the clinic gradually decreased to once every three months. She stayed in treatment for the next 20 years, progressively dealing with challenges along the way. Panic attacks returned intermittently, sometimes spontaneously and sometimes precipitated by stressors such as illness in husband or other family members, son's high school graduation, and conflict with her brothers around family inheritance. Each of these challenges caused precipitation of her symptoms and required brief periods of treatment with an antidepressant, or even a trip to the ED on one occasion. After 20 years of treatment, she was discharged from the outpatient psychiatric program and her PCP took over the prescribing of psychotropics.

Diagnostic Formulation

Aparajita's case is that of an individual suffering from Panic Disorder with Agoraphobia in the setting of several life stressors and absence of any known genetic risk factors. It is not uncommon for South Asians to struggle through anxiety with the view that it is considered a normal reaction to life events. Some even consider it a necessity that one has to go through as redemption for bad deeds in past life. Refusal to acknowledge symptoms as pathological or to recognize the need of psychiatric treatment could be due to denial and the stigma attached to having a mental illness. Other reasons include lack of vocabulary to express emotions and difficulty separating mind-body interaction. Very often South Asians tend to somaticize symptoms (e.g. backache, headache, dizziness, fatigue) or focus predominantly on physical symptoms as care from a PCP or internist – "the real doctor" – is more acceptable than care from a mental health professional. Before seeking psychiatric treatment, Aparajita had multiple visits to the ED and consultation with her PCP. Somatization may empower the person, help them make sense of life's problems, and drive away the stigma attached to a mental illness.

Aparajita taught herself braille and translated books for her disabled daughter; this underscores not only her creative problem solving skills, but also her empowerment in dealing with stress. South Asians often seek psychiatric treatment only when they are in crisis and stop care after the crisis is resolved. This can make treatment difficult, as symptoms are severe in intensity at the time of presentation. In this case, it was agoraphobia, being homebound, and an intense fear of going out that led Aparajita to seek psychiatric treatment as it interfered with her ability to provide care for her family. However, Aparajita remained compliant, stayed in treatment for more than two decades, and used the psychiatrist as her physician and life-coach for illness management and problem solving.

Aparajita's South Asian cultural background contributed to a lack of understanding of her emotional symptoms and delay in obtaining treatment. However, the cultural sanctions against alcohol and drugs were protective. Other protective factors include her intelligence, supportive spouse, absence of comorbid problems, and creative problem solving skills.

Management

Management of Aparajita's illness and contributing stressors included medications and skillfully designed therapy focusing on illness education and problem solving. Even though the psychiatrist encouraged her to work with a therapist, for reasons mentioned above (e.g. stigma, lack of insurance), she preferred to see only the psychiatrist. This is not uncommon among South Asians. Psychotherapy, or "talk therapy," is poorly understood and must be integrated into other goals of symptom management. Illness education is important as both the treatment and the prognosis depend on it. Acceptance of emotional problems as an illness does not come very easily to people from South Asia. In this case, even though Aparajita chose not to see a therapist, the psychiatrist was able to set up and provide therapy in ways that were acceptable to her. Being rigid and enforcing Western modes of therapy and treatment may not work with South Asians. Individuals may find it difficult to open up and talk about challenges in individual or group therapy. The latter can be even more intimidating as many consider sharing personal difficulties as shameful and a sign of weakness. While some patients like to take the lead and be in full control of their treatment, others like Aparajita prefer the professional to take the lead and actively problem solve. A passive stance by clinicians can be misinterpreted as either lack of interest or lack of knowledge, both of which can lead to treatment dropout.

Summary

Aparajita is a 55-year-old married female of South Asian descent who developed a long-term therapeutic relationship with the psychiatrist treating her for Panic Disorder with Agoraphobia confounded by the trauma of immigration and having a child with disabilities. Over the course of treatment, the panic attacks greatly reduced in frequency and severity. Aparajita progressively learned to identify triggers, problem solve, and actively seek help from her psychiatrist who she respected as both a physician and life coach. After 20 years of treatment, she was successfully discharged from psychiatric care and her PCP took over prescription of her psychotropic medications.

Teaching Points

1. Authority figures are respected and can be considered as coaches, teachers (e.g., gurus), or advisors. This can be used in the interest of forging the therapeutic relationship and opening the door to psychotherapy. Psychiatric diagnostic terms may not be understood, and treatment may need to be problem-oriented.

2. Emotional binds can cause conflicts, which can manifest as a psychiatric illness. The patient may feel that a pill is all that is needed to fix the problem as it can provide immediate symptom relief. South Asians may initially not be amenable to psychotherapy. It is important to gradually establish a therapeutic rapport and consider out of the box, but appropriate, strategies to improve the quality of life.
3. South Asians should be encouraged to consult social workers regarding available resources for disabled children/adults in their local community.

Gautam: Getting Family Onboard for Successful Treatment of Depression

Case History

Gautam, a 20-year-old single male college student of Asian-Indian descent, presented for psychiatric evaluation of inability to concentrate on his studies and loss of interest in day-to-day activities. He was in his second year of college at the time of the initial presentation.

Gautam was born in New Jersey to Indian parents who had immigrated to the United States (U.S.) approximately 25 years ago. The family was sponsored for immigration by a physician uncle. His parents hoped immigrating to the U.S. would provide upward psychosocial mobility and better opportunities for their children. Gautam's father, an engineer, had a well-paying job and his mother worked for a bank. After moving to the U.S., his parents had two children, first a daughter and then Gautam separated by three years.

Gautam described a happy childhood. He was raised with strict values. He was a good student but rather timid and quiet, unlike his rebellious sister. He had only one close male friend with whom he played tennis. Gautam and his sister were expected to study hard in school. They could choose to play only one sport. Over the weekends, they were expected to visit the Hindu temple and were pushed to participate in rituals and in religious classes. His parents had an active social life with other Indian immigrants but did not mingle with non-Indians outside of the work setting. Gautam and his sister were expected to socialize with the children of their parents' friends. Both were not allowed to date. Dating was interpreted by the parents as a distraction from studies. Gautam and his sister were aware of their parents' expectations: to become a doctor and have a traditional arranged marriage. Gautam's sister completed college and worked as a physical therapist, much to the disappointment of their parents.

Gautam did everything to please his parents until high school. He dated briefly, but stopped as soon as he learned of his parents' disapproval. Despite following his parents' rules, Gautam was very unhappy. He could not relate to any of the traditional values. He felt jealous of his peers who played many sports, socialized actively, and dated freely. He often felt like a social outcast. His parents and their friends called children who revolted against their belief system 'Americanized,' a rather derogatory term used in their social circle. From time to time, he blamed his situation on his parents, though he did not dare question them or openly rebel.

After graduation from high school, Gautam started studies at an Ivy League college. His parents were very happy. Gautam was excited, but also anxious, about leaving home. The college was located in a rural area and he began to feel lonely. He again had only one close friend, his roommate. He maintained a vegetarian diet, which also made him feel different. His parents visited frequently and brought him food. He did not drink alcohol or do illicit drugs. In one of his classes, he met an Indian girl, who was outgoing and smart. She encouraged him to attend social activities. He accompanied her to a dance club. Watching his peers consume alcohol and wanting to do the same evoked mixed feelings in him of confusion, guilt, and anger towards his parents for raising him with 'stupid values'. Gradually, he lost interest in everyday activities and his grades declined significantly. He attempted to obtain counseling at school but was not consistent. He felt his parents would not approve of the counseling and that the counselor would not understand his cultural conflicts.

By the end of the first semester in college, he was having anxiety and panic attacks. His family reluctantly asked a close physician friend for help. Gautam had no other medical issues. He was not on any medications. His family history was negative for psychiatric illness. The physician friend of the family suggested psychiatric evaluation and treatment. At first, the family was embarrassed and reluctant to have their son see a psychiatrist preferring to see a temple priest, or seek Ayurveda or homeopathic treatment instead. His family was clearly concerned about the stigma mental illness carried. Later, they reluctantly agreed to see a psychiatrist, as Gautam's mental health continued to decline.

At the initial visit, the psychiatrist obtained Gautam's permission for evaluation and treatment. The psychiatrist spent extra time on this since the appointment call was made by a close friend of the family. The psychiatrist also got consent for involving the family during the treatment. Gautam readily agreed and expressed his happiness about working with a specialist. He was, however, unsure if his family was onboard but hoped they would be. With his permission, the psychiatrist spoke to each family member (mother, father and sister) as a group and individually. The psychiatrist outlined the evaluation and treatment process. At first, the family seemed skeptical about medications and regular visits. After being educated about Gautam's symptoms, and that they were probably related to a brain condition rather than a character weakness, the family agreed to treatment.

Diagnostic Formulation

Gautam reported a six-month history of persistent sadness, lack of joy, decreased motivation, feelings of hopelessness, and a decrease in sleep, energy, and concentration. He also reported intermittent symptoms of anxiety and panic attacks. He had no self-destructive thoughts and no homicidal ideation. He was diagnosed as having Major Depressive Disorder and started on a selective serotonin reuptake inhibitor. The psychiatrist also recommended weekly individual talk therapy and family therapy.

At the individual and family therapy sessions, the psychiatrist learned of the cultural factors associated with triggering Gautam's depressive and anxiety symptoms. These factors included Gautam's love and respect for his parents but his inability to understand their rigidity with South Asian cultural values and their inflexibility to adapt to Western culture despite living in the U.S. for 25 years. Major stressors included having to socialize with only children of parents attending the Hindu temple, involvement in only religious social activities, not dating, playing only a single sport, and complete abstinence from alcohol. Although Gautam would occasionally chose to do things differently (e.g., dating, visiting clubs), he could not maintain these changes out of fear that his family would reject him. As a result, he felt like a social outcast with neither friends from his background nor non-Indian friends. He was afraid of being labeled 'Americanized' by his family. His introverted personality traits and passive aggressive behavior also contributed to his difficulties in being assertive. His emotional state, fluctuating between anger and guilt, precipitated and maintained his depression.

Management

Management was multipronged and included a combination of medication and psychotherapy. In addition to individual therapy, treatment also focused on getting the family onboard, educating them respectfully, and addressing their concerns. It was clear that support and approval from family was important to Gautam. The psychiatrist reassured the family that Gautam's condition could be treated with a medication. Although his sister and mother agreed, his father had many questions about the medicine. The psychiatrist patiently answered his questions. In addition to meeting with all the family members as a group, the psychiatrist chose to meet with each one of them separately (with Gautam's consent), which helped establish a therapeutic rapport and garner full support of Gautam's treatment.

Gautam remained compliant with treatment. Educating him about Major Depressive Disorder as a brain illness played an important role in his medication compliance. His depressive symptoms improved with antidepressant titration. With weekly psychotherapy, Gautam gradually spoke more about psychosocial and cultural stressors with the psychiatrist. It was revealed that Gautam's family issues were a major source of stress for him. He viewed his father as controlling and his mother as subdued. Gautam identified with his mother, became timid, and never fought back when his father expected him to follow his cultural values. He resented his parents for stifling his 'American' identity. On the other hand, he was afraid of losing his family and being away from them caused incredible stress. His emotional state fluctuated between anger and guilt. It was obvious that he loved and respected his parents, but he also struggled to attain independence and develop bicultural values. Therapy focused on empowering him to take control of his life and make his own decisions. The psychiatrist helped him accept his family's cultural values while developing his own identity and values. Over time, he was comfortable having a bicultural identity. He began to openly express his feelings with his family without feelings of guilt.

The psychiatrist also met with his parents and sister individually and as a group. His parents were concerned about family reputation being influenced by Gautam's mental illness diagnosis. This education included comparing mental illness to a chronic medical illness such as diabetes, which the family found beneficial and easy to understand. They had great difficulty understanding the reason for regular talk therapy and preferred visiting occasionally with a temple priest. The psychiatrist accepted with respect their traditional views about ayurvedic and homeopathic medicines and their faith in the priest and reinforced the importance of hopefulness and faith in recovery. The psychiatrist highlighted that even though ayurvedic and homeopathic treatments may have therapeutic potential, they have not been scientifically studied. This resonated well with Gautam's parents who valued science and research. Gradually the family accepted the diagnosis and treatment plan and supported Gautam through his treatment and recovery.

On a combination of medications, regular psychotherapy, and intermittent visits with a temple priest, Gautam made significant progress. After completing his undergraduate degree, he found work at an organization of his choice. He learned to recognize relapses and identify triggers associated with his illness. He was able to openly discuss his issues of dependency and his passive aggressive behavior. Although he was not married, he had meaningful relationships with females and hoped to marry in the future. His relationship with his parents and sister improved. His parents have accepted that mental illness can be treated and that the stigma should not prevent anyone from obtaining treatment.

Summary

Gautam is a 20-year-old single male undergraduate student of Asian-Indian descent who presented with symptoms of Major Depressive Disorder in the context of several psychosocial stressors, predominantly related to his strict upbringing and strong family cultural values. Management was multipronged and included a combination of a medication and psychotherapy. In addition to individual therapy, treatment also focused on getting the family onboard, educating them respectfully, and addressing their concerns.

Teaching Points

1. Psychiatrists and therapists may be contacted by family friends regarding referrals of other friends and family. It is important to talk to the patient prior to the evaluation and obtain consent for evaluation, treatment, and working with the family.
2. Meeting with family members, individually and as a group, is important as they often have tremendous influence on the patient. It is possible that without establishing a trusting relationship with the family, patients will not be compliant with treatment.
3. The value of taking psychotropics for chronic depression is important and analogies with taking medicines for other chronic medical conditions may help with acceptance and compliance.
4. It is important for clinicians to provide mental illness education and address stigma, but also be openminded about traditional values and beliefs. These values and believes can often provide a safe, non-invasive complement to the treatment plan.

Shyam: Treating the Complex Interplay of Mania, Psychosis, and Acculturation with a Multipronged Approach

Case History

Shyam, a 37-year-old married male of South Asian descent, was seen in an outpatient psychiatry clinic shortly after his third psychiatric hospitalization. He carried a diagnosis of Bipolar Affective Disorder, Type 1, with Psychosis.

Shyam was born in a remote rural town in Southern India. His birth and early development were normal. He was the second of four children and the oldest son. He and his siblings were raised in a poor, but loving, environment. Shyam's father drove auto rickshaws (a motorized three-wheeler) and his mother was a homemaker. There were no known health or behavior problems in his childhood. He did well in school and earned an engineering degree. Shyam did not smoke tobacco, drink alcohol, or use illicit drugs. He had no known medical problems. Family history was positive for psychiatric illness on both sides of his family. A maternal great uncle and cousin had committed suicide with further details unclear. A maternal aunt had an unknown psychiatric illness. Two paternal uncles suffered from alcohol dependence.

Being the oldest son, Shyam was expected to share in the financial responsibilities of the family at an early age. He tutored other students as early as age 13 and continued to do so through college. Opportunities in his hometown were limited, and Shyam attended an engineering college several hundred miles away. He would visit his family only a couple of times each year. After graduating from college, Shyam was offered a job in the Middle East. Although it was his first time living outside India, he felt reasonably supported, as the same company had also recruited many of his peers. He lived in a dorm-style housing unit and spent all of his free time with his peers. He initially had no trouble socializing with his peers or other colleagues / supervisors at work.

As the weeks went by, however, Shyam became increasingly suspicious of his colleagues and about the larger society around him. Gradually, he became hyper-religious and developed an elaborate set of ritualistic behaviors. During this time, many of his peers were accepting new jobs in Europe or the United States (U.S.). Shyam eventually applied and got a job in Minneapolis as an IT consultant. The company promised to obtain legal status for him. Despite this, the transition to living and working in the U.S. was extremely difficult for him. He found the winters very cold and unbearable. He had no family or friends in Minneapolis and felt very lonely. He spoke English with a heavy accent and others had great difficulty understanding him. This led to bullying by coworkers and peers. He felt rejected by them, which enhanced his sense of isolation. Even the local Indian temple gave him little comfort. It was a North Indian temple with different rituals and customs in contrast to the South Indian temples he was accustomed to.

Less than a year after his move to the U.S., at the age of 29, Shyam had his first episode of mania with psychosis. Symptoms included elated mood with intermittent anger outbursts, poor sleep, increased energy, and racing thoughts. He had prominent delusions as follows: (1) paranoid delusions of coworkers conspiring against him, (2) persecutory delusions of police being after him to deport him back to India, (3) grandiose delusions of being a stock market genius, and (4) religious delusions of being the savior. He also experienced several physical symptoms such as dizziness, pressure in his head, chest discomfort, restlessness, and difficulty sitting still. At work, he often became angry and argumentative at meetings. He was initially referred to his company's Employee Assistance Program (EAP) counselor, who recommended that he should go to the nearest emergency department. He followed the counselor's suggestion and was admitted voluntarily to the psychiatry unit of a local hospital. After a one-week admission, he was discharged on medications in a stable state with the diagnosis of Bipolar Affective Disorder, Type 1, most recent episode manic, with psychotic features. He initially took his medications, but began to miss doses. He was reluctant to seek psychotherapy. He believed his symptoms were related to his poor physical health or "body weakness" and felt it was "karma" to endure the suffering. He continued to have residual symptoms of mild paranoia and grandiosity.

Two years later, Shyam moved to Atlanta. Although this was another disruption, he had become somewhat acclimated to the American way of life. While he was in Atlanta, his parents from India visited him and learned of his hospitalization. He presented it to them as a "hospitalization for check-up of body weaknesses." His parents encouraged him to get married, as they believed having a spouse would improve his "body weakness." Shyam was also open to the idea of marriage. He met a girl on an Indian dating website and married her soon after. The problems in their marriage started almost immediately. His wife was from Northern India and had a professional, urban background. She also worked in the IT field and earned more than Shyam. She was resentful of Shyam financially supporting his parents, as they were trying to establish themselves as a new couple. This lead to frequent fights between them. Shyam felt torn between his wife's objections and his parents' demands. Shyam began to drink alcohol quite heavily, which created more friction. Gradually, his emotional health deteriorated and he was psychiatrically admitted for another manic episode with psychosis. He was discharged with recommendations to continue his medications and seek outpatient psychiatric care. He was again intermittently compliant with medications and never followed through on the recommendation to establish outpatient care. He still held on to his theory of "body weakness" and the need to undergo suffering in this life as redemption for evil deeds in his past life.

The marital strife continued. In addition, the couple was unable to conceive a child. As a result, fertility treatment was recommended, which was very expensive. Shyam's wife became increasingly frustrated with his financial support of his parents and retaliated by quitting her job. Under these stressors, he experienced his third episode of mania with psychosis. He was hospitalized a third time, this time for a couple of weeks. A key difference following discharge was that he agreed to seek outpatient care, with his wife in full agreement.

Diagnostic Formulation

Shyam likely had a genetic propensity to develop a mood disorder based on the strong family history of psychiatric illness. In addition, he faced other stressors: living in two different foreign countries, marital strife, financial challenges, and fertility issues. The move to the U.S. was the most difficult one and caused significant emotional stress. He had great difficulty with acculturation. Shyam's hyper-religiosity, which had already started prior to his move to the U.S., was ego-syntonic for him, as he believed his regular prayers to God made him a savior. In addition, he did not see his paranoid ideas as being pathological. He thought he was protecting himself of foreigners by being extremely cautious and questioning their behaviors. The different stressors debilitated him of his resources. Shyam's psychiatric decompensation appeared to be a perfect storm.

Management

Shyam's outpatient psychiatric care with a psychologist and a psychiatrist began after discharge from his third hospitalization. By this time, he was on a stable medication regimen and was compliant with his medications. The psychologist focused on providing support, hope, and different forms of therapy to help him cope and adjust to his illness. At the time of initial evaluation, a detailed psychosocial history was obtained and a treatment plan was formulated with Shyam's input. Shyam liked being in control and appreciated the therapist's suggestion of taking responsibility for his care. Together they devised a plan, which included:

- Psychoeducation about his illness and medications, including identifying triggers and importance of compliance
- Problem solving specific issues (e.g., conflict with co-workers, conflict with family members, money management)
- Family therapy to improve better communication with his wife
- Referral to the local chapter of the National Alliance For Mental Illness (NAMI), which had a peer-to-peer group for South Asians

- Engaging in prosocial activities and an exercise regimen
- Relapse prevention and maintenance therapy

The treatment team initially placed Shyam on medical leave for six weeks to monitor his symptoms and medications. However, at the end of this period, he had not sufficiently recovered to return to work. He was then placed on short-term disability for an additional six weeks. At his request, he was referred to an Indian psychiatrist. Even though neither his psychiatrist nor the psychologist spoke Shyam's native language, they were closely aligned with his cultural background, which helped him trust and confide in them. With his written consent, the therapist stayed in regular touch with his psychiatrist and even his primary care provider to ensure that Shyam remained medically stable and all his clinicians were informed of his progress.

Shyam reported that he did not feel understood by prior treating clinicians as they lacked his cultural background, were "too strict," and he felt insulted by how little they knew about India. He reported this as a main reason for never seeking outpatient psychotherapy. He felt comfortable having an Indian psychiatrist and psychologist. Shyam had never met any other South Asians with his issues. The few times he had had any conversation about mental illness with his peers, they were shaming. A big challenge for the psychologist was trying to dispel the stigma of mental illness with both Shyam and his family. At first Shyam denied mental illness, stating his weak body was trying to adjust to a new environment and / or that it was his karma. He quoted situations from religious books and South Asian TV shows to explain his symptoms and the need to silently endure them. He believed the suffering was necessary and could not be eliminated by talk therapy or medications, but by prayers, rituality, and self-discipline. The therapist patiently listened to his theories of illness and supplemented them with facts on mental illness based on research and science. She did not contradict or devalue his explanations. As he learned more about the biological factors associated with his illness, he became compliant with his medications and more open about discussing his symptoms. He learned to recognize that many of his somatic symptoms were part of his mental illness. Eventually he was able to explain his illness to his parents without ascribing any blame to himself or to them.

Shyam's wife also actively participated in the therapy sessions. She was amenable to discussing the issues that she had with Shyam and his family. They mostly revolved around finances. She felt comfortable that the psychologist was Indian and therefore could understood the "in-law problems" that many Indian women have. She was greatly relieved to hear that the psychologist was not recommending divorce. They were even able to joke about the well-known "saas-bahu" (mother-in-law and daughter-in-law) soaps on Indian TV. Shyam's wife became a strong ally in his treatment. She eventually came to see his psychologist and psychiatrist as coaches and guides. When available, Shyam's parents were also included in the therapy sessions. The psychologist used various strategies to provide psychoeducation and problem solve. Religious values were discussed with chapters from well-known religious books and appropriate video clips used. Books, including workbooks on mental illness authored by professionals and non-professionals, were recommended. Shyam and his family were encouraged to attend support groups. Also beneficial was providing analogies to other medical conditions.

Shyam recovered well and returned to work. After the initial 12-week course of active treatment, which involved seeing him weekly, he was transitioned to every other week for four months. He was monitored closely during his first month back at work. Once he proved to be stable, the visits were tapered to once every three weeks and ultimately every three months.

Summary

Shyam is a 37-year-old married male of South Asian descent with a positive family history of psychiatric illness and a personal history of bipolar disorder with psychotic features who required both inpatient and outpatient treatment. His illness was precipitated and maintained by several factors: non-compliance with psychiatric treatment, intermittent alcohol use, acculturation challenges, marital strife, and financial stress. In addition, his limited insight into his illness and tendency to somaticize hindered his recovery. With appropriate culturally sensitive psychiatric treatment, he made good recovery on a combination of medications and psychotherapy. His initial reluctance to stay in treatment gradually resolved with an appropriate cultural view of illness, learning more about his illness and related triggers, accepting the importance of consistent treatment, and recognizing the love and support from his wife.

Teaching Points

1. Ignorance and stigma about mental illness run deep in South Asian communities, despite high levels of education in many of them. Educating these individuals about mental illness and giving opportunities to ask questions are important aspects of treatment.

2. In addition to usual treatment approaches (e.g., psychoeducation, medications, individual therapy, couples therapy), it is important to determine other cultural strategies that may be well received by the patient. In this case, use of vignettes and examples from television serials and religious books helped consolidate the therapeutic relationship between the psychologist, psychiatrist, the patient, and his wife, which ultimately paved the way for successful recovery.

Manoj: Unanswered Questions after Completed Suicide in an Elderly Man

Case History

Manoj, a 70-year-old married male who was born and lived in India, was treated by an outpatient psychiatrist for Dysthymia. He was treated by two different psychiatrists over the years with the first moving to the United States (U.S.) and handing off care to the second. The first psychiatrist, who wrote this report, spoke to the patient a few additional times after discontinuation of care.

Manoj's birth and early development were normal. He lost his father at the age of five. He was raised in a loving environment by his mother and extended maternal family members. He excelled throughout his education and graduated with an engineering degree in India. He started a construction company in his 20s, which did fairly well. He was married at age 25 by an arranged marriage. He did not drink alcohol or abuse other illicit substances. His medical history was insignificant except that he suffered from chronic depression from age 25 onwards.

Although he did not personally endorse symptoms of depression, he preferred to stay aloof, rarely socialized with any friends, and preferred to read in his free time. After his marriage, his wife noticed that he was dull, uninterested, and distant from family and friends. His sleep was poor, and he had difficulty concentrating. She asked him repeatedly to see a physician. However, he chose not to discuss his emotional condition with family, friends, or even his physician. He was concerned about the negative effect it would have on family reputation. He would often say, "this is my Karma", suggesting it was his fate to suffer. His business continued to do well because he had a loyal manager who he depended on. He was aware that he was not able to develop his business to its full potential. Despite this, he took time to participate in community activities and volunteer in several organizations.

Ultimately, he visited a psychiatrist at the insistence of his wife and mother. The psychiatrist diagnosed chronic persistent depression (Dysthymia) and started him on an antidepressant. In addition to taking the medication, he also started the practice of meditation and yoga. After a year of treatment, his mood improved. He was convinced that it was yoga and meditation, and not the antidepressant that had helped. His relationship with his wife improved; they had a daughter and fondly raised her together. He continued to see his psychiatrist once every few months and took the antidepressant only intermittently. During his visits with the psychiatrist, he discussed his Jain religion and his beliefs in karma, previous births, and reincarnation. His wife also accompanied him for some of these visits. There were no overt symptoms of clinical depression, psychosis, or other symptoms of major mental illness. As time passed, his psychiatrist immigrated to the U.S. and referred him to another psychiatrist in India. His daughter, now an adult, married and moved to the U.S. with her husband.

Manoj had great difficulty accepting these changes; however, he continued to see the new psychiatrist. He explained to him that his "bad karma" in his previous lives was causing his current suffering and that medications would not help. He refused to take any medicines prescribed by the new psychiatrist, but continued to see him quarterly. The sessions predominantly focused on his religious values, such as need for suffering in present life to negate the effect of bad karma. He spoke of the importance of making sacrifices to attain nirvana – a state of reunion with God after cycling through life and death. He also spoke of euthanasia in which he strongly believed. However, he neither discussed the nature of his bad karma nor expressed interest in exploring it further, even when questioned. He continued yoga and meditation, and started other enjoyable activities such as painting, learning religious music, and studying his Jain religion in great depth.

His mother and wife accepted his lifestyle. As he was functional and productive, they supported him in being medication free. Manoj and his wife visited their daughter in the U.S. frequently, and these visits usually lifted his spirits. At what would be his last visit to the U.S., at the age of 70, he seemed to be in a good mood. He helped his son-in-law around the house. He went on trips with his daughter's family and enjoyed playing with his grandchildren. He discussed medical topics such as euthanasia with his daughter and son-in-law. He was in favor of euthanasia and disappointed that it was illegal in India. Manoj decided to return to India earlier than his wife as his 90-year-old mother was staying by herself. Manoj's wife was staying longer to help her daughter's family with a new baby. Two days prior to his departure, he had a pleasant telephone conversation with his previous psychiatrist, who was living in the U.S. He also had seemingly normal conversations with a few of his friends and acquaintances in the U.S.

On his day of arrival to India, he had dinner with his mother and went to bed. There was no evidence of sadness or distress; his mother was very happy to see him calm and relaxed. The next morning he took a shower, dressed himself in clean white clothes, gave his mother a warm hug, touched her feet to ask for her blessings, and went into his room. He requested the housekeeper not to disturb him, as he was jetlagged and needed to rest. Several hours passed. His mother and the housekeeper noticed that he had missed lunch and he would miss dinner if they did not wake him up. The housekeeper knocked on his door several times and finally pushed open the door forcefully. To everyone's shock, Manoj had hung himself by tying the bedsheet to the ceiling fan. His prayer book was open. The bedsheet was tied to the fan, and he had gagged himself. There was no suicide note.

As expected, the family was devastated. However, they took comfort in that his last days were spent lovingly with family and that he had obtained his mother's blessing prior to his death. His wife called his sudden death "a brain attack just like a heart attack." His wife and family were not angry or bitter with the psychiatrist. They appreciated the support that was given to him at all times and the respect the doctors had for his values and belief system.

Diagnostic Formulation

Manoj experienced chronic depression starting from age 25, which was partially treated. Despite lingering symptoms, he was productive and functional. He managed his business with the help of a dedicated and competent manager. He had no medical problems. He had a loving family and a comfortable lifestyle. He self-explained his chronic depression as his karma; that because of certain deeds in his past life he was destined to live with a sense of void and inner suffering. He truly believed that there was no treatment for his suffering except for doing good deeds in this life, which would build good karma for his next birth. Manoj believed in euthanasia and felt that every person has the right to choose to die. However, he did not endorse feelings of hopelessness or suicidal thoughts. He never used terms such as sadness or depression to describe his mood.

Culturally, as a practicing Jain, Manoj believed suffering in this life was based on karma (i.e., the impact of deeds in his previous life). He accepted his suffering and never questioned or blamed anyone for it. He also believed in reincarnation. He did good deeds by participating in community events and doing charitable work to have a better next life. Asian-Indians who believe in Jain religion are convinced that their fate and destiny are pre-written. Based on this religious/spiritual thinking, his family was able to take solace although they realized that there will always be unanswered questions.

Management

Establishing rapport through understanding the unique cultural aspect of a patient's belief system is the cornerstone of successful treatment. The key ingredients for building strong rapport include clinician characteristics such as honesty, respecting the individual's values and beliefs, and non-judgmentally accepting patients for who they are. The therapeutic relationship with Manoj greatly improved when the clinician was able to identify and make use of Manoj's strength: his strong religious beliefs. He felt valued and supported when the psychiatrist approved strategies such as yoga, meditation, and spiritual psychotherapy rather than medications.

Manoj found talking to his clinician a less stigmatizing and acceptable strategy to cope with day-to-day life. The painting and music lessons also helped reduce his sense of void and emptiness.

Acceptance of emotional problems as an illness does not come very easily to Indian patients, as evidenced by Manoj's unhappiness to be treated for emotional problems. Culturally, Indian men are conditioned from the time they are little boys to "hold it all in" and not show anything that can be perceived as weakness. He was reluctant to seek treatment because of beliefs that medications or therapy can do little to change his situation. In addition, reluctance was also secondary to stigma, shame, and embarrassment. These concerns are often deep rooted in the Asian-Indian culture. Providing education about mental illness in an honest, non-judgmental way, and involving family, is the best way to address stigma and shame.

Although Manoj's suicide will never be understood, many Asian-Indians do not consider death final. They believe in rebirth and in reincarnation. They believe the soul is immortal and after death, the soul goes through the cycle of rebirth. These values help in conceptualizing death as not the end, but a continuation of the journey towards nirvana. Supportive therapy sessions with Manoj and his wife, when she attended, focused on the meaning of life and importance of sacrifice to achieve "moksha," which is liberation of the soul from the cycle of rebirth and attainment of unity with the Supreme Being. Manoj found these sessions fulfilling and therapeutic. However, there will always be unanswered questions of why Manoj committed suicide and if this could have been prevented. Should the doctors have forced him to take antidepressants and could this have prevented the suicide? Could exploring in-depth his beliefs on his past life and bad karma have reduced his suffering and prevented suicide?

Summary

Manoj was a married 70-year-old Indian male with strong belief in the Jain religion and euthanasia, and a past psychiatric history of Dysthymia from early adulthood, who completed suicide via hanging. He chose to participate in psychiatric treatment in a manner that he found useful and comforting. He was deeply religious and strongly believed in karma and reincarnation. He meticulously planned his death and killed himself after obtaining blessings from his mother and saying goodbye to his family and friends. His family members have accepted his death as a "sudden brain attack." His clinicians, however, will always wonder if they had done enough or if they should have done more to prevent his death.

Teaching Points

1. Patients with chronic depression may not always report sadness, unhappiness, or low mood. They may present with a sense of void and be unable to experience pleasure. It is important to probe deeper and obtain collateral history from family.
2. Suffering is valued and considered the norm or part of karma in many religious patients. As such, patients are often reluctant to seek help with a fear that the clinician will not understand their ways of thinking and may judge them.
3. Clinicians must finely balance respecting patients' cultural and religious values with maintaining safety and being aggressive with treatment.
4. In the setting of a patient suicide, clinicians may be left with unanswered questions and guilt. In this case, the question of whether an antidepressant may have prevented suicide will go unanswered.
5. Family members must also come to terms with a completed suicide. In this case, the family found closure with understanding that Manoj had a "brain attack."

Arun: "Bad" Behavior as a Sign of Schizophrenia

Case History

Arun, a 16-year-old male born in the United States (U.S.) to Bengali parents, was evaluated in a comprehensive and multi-disciplinary outpatient mental health clinic for treatment of schizophrenia.

Arun's parents were born and raised in India, where they had an arranged marriage. Arun's father was a teacher in India and his mother barely had a high school education. Arun's parents immigrated to the U.S. as a young couple. They resided with Arun's paternal uncle and his family. This was a stressful period, as Arun's mother did not get along very well with her sister-in-law who was unkind and resented their presence in the home. Arun's father was unable to continue working as a teacher in the U.S. and worked at a gas station while his mother was a homemaker. After two years, the couple became self-sufficient enough to move out of the uncle's home.

Arun's parents had two children: Arun and his younger sister. Arun was the product of an unremarkable pregnancy and delivery. His developmental milestones were met on time and he was healthy. The family struggled financially, but managed on his father's income, who worked very long and hard hours. Although relationships with extended family members became further strained, the family had met other Bengalis and would occasionally socialize with them.

When Arun was four years old, his father died suddenly and unexpectedly from a heart attack. Arun's mother was left to care for two young children on her own. Due to financial reasons, her family was unable to come to the U.S. to assist. She did receive some support and guidance from friends and acquaintances, but not for long. The owner of the gas station where her husband had worked for a few years was especially kind to her and provided her with some job training. She was able to secure employment at the same gas station with various responsibilities, such as stocking and arranging the shelves and managing the cash register.

Arun managed to function reasonably well through elementary school. Although only an average student, he did not have any behavioral difficulties at school. Around age fourteen, he began missing classes and became fearful of attending school because he believed his peers and teachers were against him, even though there was no evidence to support this. He would refuse to go to the cafeteria during lunchtime or eat school lunches due to concerns that the food was dirty and mixed with urine and feces by his peers. When school staff attempted to redirect or reassure him, he became irritable and accused staff of colluding with the other students.

At home, Arun was increasingly withdrawn to his room. He would hide under the covers, talk to himself, and make punching gestures in the air. He avoided taking showers complaining that the shower water was dirty and that someone in the shower was punching him, talking "garbage" about him, and pulling on his hair. Some nights, he complained of having trouble sleeping, and he would check in his closet and behind his furniture to ensure that no one was hiding in his room.

During this time, his school made frequent attempts to contact his mother, but his mother avoided answering these calls due to a language barrier. She would rely on Arun's sister, who spoke English and Bengali, to speak with the school and then explain to her what was going on. These calls would infuriate Arun's mother, who would accuse Arun of bad behavior. Arun became increasingly aggressive, including pushing his mother, punching walls, and hitting his sister when she tried to intervene. The neighbors contacted law enforcement due to the episodes of yelling and screaming, and his mother received a warning from the landlord about possible eviction. Arun was never arrested and had no history of substance use. Arun was usually apologetic for his behaviors, but insisted that people were against him and that no one understood.

At age 15, Arun had five involuntary psychiatric hospitalizations over the course of one year. These were initiated by school or law enforcement, due to his aggressive outbursts and bizarre statements and behaviors. Arun's mother had never met with any of the hospital psychiatrists, and any communication she had with the hospital was with a social worker who would primarily speak with Arun's sister. The hospital would provide prescriptions and discharge instructions with a list of the prescribed medications, follow-up appointments, and multiple names and numbers of outpatient resources. Arun did not keep his follow-up appointments or take his medications following any of the first four hospitalizations.

Following his fifth admission, Arun was referred to a different outpatient community mental health center that included a social worker that met with the family at home within the first week following discharge. His assigned psychiatrist was an Indo-American child psychiatrist who also spoke a little Bengali. Arun was diagnosed with schizophrenia based on his symptoms of paranoid / persecutory delusions, auditory hallucinations, disorganized and illogical thought processes, and inappropriate behaviors. These symptoms were significantly influencing his social and academic functioning. The psychiatrist spent many sessions educating the mother and sister about schizophrenia and the importance of consistent treatment. Arun was on three different oral medications, and his sister related that it was a battle getting Arun to take his pills. His medication regimen was simplified to a single long-acting injectable (depot) antipsychotic medication to facilitate medication adherence. He and his family were provided with coordinated care, counseling services, school accommodations, case management, and other supportive interventions. One and half years later, Arun was overall stable, had not had any significant aggressive incidents or active symptoms of psychosis, had been able to remain out of the hospital, and with accommodations in place, was able to attend school consistently.

Diagnostic Formulation

Arun presented initially with disruptive behavior at school, a major concern for his mother. She perceived him as disobedient and disruptive, would get angry when the school contacted her, and directed her focus on disciplining him rather than further trying to understand what may be triggering such behaviors. She experienced disappointment that her son was not like his sister, who was well behaved and a good student. Culturally, her lack of awareness of mental health problems, her inadequate education, and social pressures of being a single parent may have contributed to her inability to identify and perceive the signals of mental health difficulties.

Arun's psychotic symptoms were negatively affecting his academic and social functioning. Although there may have been some teasing and bullying at school, he was unable to recognize that his beliefs were irrational. His outbursts jeopardized the family's stability, led to threats of eviction, and resulted in psychiatric hospitalizations. His mother failed to recognize his symptoms as being derived from a mental illness and never sought guidance from friends due to embarrassment over his behaviors.

Socially, the family lacked adequate support systems. Arun's mother, a single parent and sole provider with low-income employment, was often confused and overwhelmed by her son's behaviors. Her daughter had to take on additional responsibilities as interpreter, liaison, and caretaker. His mother had little formal education, lacked knowledge of mental illness, and sought minimal support from extended family or friends. Cultural factors, such as a language barrier, contributed to frequent breakdown in maintaining treatment despite several psychiatric hospitalizations.

Management

Minority groups are more likely to delay seeking treatment until symptoms are more severe and are less inclined to seek treatment from mental health specialists. Arun did not receive any services early in the course of his illness, and his first encounter with treatment was when he was involuntarily hospitalized. Despite multiple subsequent hospitalizations, consistent follow-up and maintenance of treatment did not occur. There were several contributory factors to this lack of successful follow-up: poor communication between clinicians and family, family's lack of knowledge on mental illness, wrongly directed focus on behavior rather than illness, poor support systems, and inefficient linkage to appropriate treatment services.

Establishing rapport played a significant role in accomplishing treatment adherence. Both Arun and his mother instantly felt comfortable upon seeing a psychiatrist of Indian origin. The psychiatrist had partial fluency of the Bengali language and utilized commonality of language as a tool to connect with the family. The psychiatrist brought up ethnic music that Arun and his family were familiar with (e.g., Rabindra Sangeet) during the first appointment, which seemed to break down some of the barriers and reduce tension. Other common ethnic interests, such as Bollywood movies, were periodically discussed. Arun took great pleasure in making movie recommendations to the psychiatrist. In short, Arun and his family were able to make a cultural connection with the psychiatrist.

A strategic decision to assign a case manager of South Asian origin to work with the family was made to make more personal. The case manager made home visits, and this was less intimidating to the family, who did not have to worry about what was playing on TV or what cooking smells were emanating when a visit was made. The case manager accompanied the family to school meetings and helped facilitate communication with school personnel for procurement of specialized school services and accommodations. The case manager also helped initiate the application for Arun's disability benefits and helped the family access resources, such as free school supplies.

Arun also had a Caucasian therapist who made home visits. The therapist utilized the psychiatrist and case manager's cultural connection with the family to establish rapport. Her initial meeting with Arun and his family was during a psychiatric follow-up appointment at the office, and the psychiatrist introduced the therapist to the family, explained the therapist's role on the team, and reassured Arun's mother that she could contact the psychiatrist at any time if she had any questions. She worked with Arun on anger management strategies, identifying triggers, seeking appropriate diversion resources, resilience building, psycho-education, and the importance of medication adherence.

Complex pharmacotherapy was a reason for medication non-adherence in Arun's case. This was compounded by a lack of psycho-education in Arun's mother. Arun's resistance towards taking the medications made it even more difficult to maintain consistency in treatment. Starting a long-acting injectable antipsychotic, and stopping oral medications, helped with medication adherence. Arun felt more comfortable having monthly injections rather than taking daily pills. This also removed the daily conflicts and power struggles over medication administration within the home.

Illness education was of paramount importance in this case. A focus was helping Arun's mother understand that Arun's "bad behavior" was a symptom of schizophrenia and not always a willful attempt to be disobedient. Arun's sister was encouraged to seek resources about schizophrenia and to ask questions, which she did. This was very beneficial as the sister, despite being very young, was the stabilizing force in the family and a proxy parent. It was important for her to understand why her brother was "acting" this way, to be acknowledged for the role that she had assumed, and to be validated that she had her own needs to maintain wellbeing.

Summary

Arun is a 16-year-old single male born in the U.S. to Bengali parents with onset of schizophrenia at a young age who required several psychiatric hospitalizations before appropriate, comprehensive outpatient treatment was successfully arranged. Various cultural and social factors contributed to barriers in initiation and continuation of treatment. His untreated mental illness and its consequences created great stress within the family. A multimodal treatment approach provided by a team that was culturally able to connect with the family lead to positive treatment outcomes and improvement in the quality of life for Arun and his family.

Teaching Points

1. It can be difficult to recognize psychosis in children as the focus may be placed on disruptive behaviors. Most Indian parents who have immigrated to the U.S. expect their children to be respectful to elders and be star performers at school. Hence, any disruptive behaviors and poor academic performance brings shame and humiliation. It is important for clinicians to educate parents that disruptive behavior could be a symptom of a more serious mental health condition.

2. Psychotic symptoms and untreated mental illness cause disruption across a teenager's life, from school to friends and family. Children who are racially and ethnically diverse are more likely to experience bullying, an added stressor, which further compromises their emotional stability. In addition to educating families, clinicians may also have to work with teachers and school authorities to educate them about mental illness so they can prevent bullying and serve as first responders.

3. Identifying and utilizing cultural commonalities to establish a cultural connection can facilitate therapeutic alliance. Establishing rapport with culturally aligned mental health professionals could be highly effective in promoting treatment adherence.

Ravi: Obsessive Compulsive Symptoms and Hidden Sexual Identity

Case History

Ravi, a 25-year-old single Asian-Indian male working as a computer programmer, was referred to an outpatient psychiatrist for management of anxiety, aggression, and obsessive-compulsive symptoms. He was referred by his primary care physician, a friend of his family, to an Asian-Indian psychiatrist familiar with Hindu culture and the Tamil language.

Ravi had been in his usual state of good health until approximately a year prior to initial consultation. At that time, and seemingly for no apparent reason, his parents reported that he became focused on cleanliness. He began to take showers several times a day. He began cleaning his kitchen counter frequently, even if it had not been used. His family noticed that he often would re-start chores and projects for no apparent reason. For example, the family noticed he threw out a salad he was preparing three times as the knife may be contaminated. Another aspect of his behavior that drew the attention of the family was the frequency of his angry outbursts following political arguments. In the past Ravi, a liberal, would often argue with his conservative parents, but with humor and good-natured teasing thrown in. However, during the primary season of the 2016 election, when the family would watch TV together, the arguments became loud. In what was atypical for him, Ravi became abusive. He cursed, threw objects, insulted his parents and his younger sister, and often would walk out of the house. Occasionally he called back to apologize. More often he returned a few days later and did not mention the event.

Ravi became more involved with religion and religious activities. He began praying frequently. He began reciting mantras prior to various activities, such as leaving home or boarding a train. He had specific and strict rules, such as chanting the mantra 108 times. If he doubted that he had counted accurately, he would start over.

His family was aware and concerned about these changes and initially felt paralyzed and powerless. However, they were driven to action following a change in Ravi's eating habits. He gradually began to avoid certain spices and then certain foods. His list of foods that were taboo grew over time. He also started to fast one day a week, to purify himself. Later, he increased the fasting to two days a week. He began to look gaunt and lost over 20 pounds.

The parents finally called their family physician, a close friend of the family, who had known Ravi since birth. The family physician was well liked by Ravi and his sisters who all referred to him as Doctor Uncle. He met Ravi in his home and was taken aback with the changes he noticed. Ravi acknowledged the changes and even agreed that these may be abnormal and excessive but felt powerless. He confided in his physician that he had "bad" thoughts that he was "impure and tainted" and had to respond to them with rituals that brought him relief. He also reported that he had intrusive thoughts and images of violent and tragic accidents happening to his parents and sisters. These images involved fatal accidents, as well as physical and sexual assaults to his loved ones. These were alleviated only if he said the appropriate prayers or conducted the 'right' type of prayers – 'Pooja'.

The family physician referred Ravi to an experienced and respected Caucasian psychiatrist. Ravi saw this psychiatrist a few times, but was dissatisfied with the experience. He felt deceived that the psychiatrist answered his questions with questions. He felt the psychiatrist was "cold, aloof and uncaring" and did not understand him. Ravi was particularly upset that he had to explain various terms and concepts pertaining to the Hindu religion (e.g. Gayathri Japam, Arti, Prasad, and Pooja) to the Caucasian psychiatrist. Ravi's father was angry because the psychiatrist would not meet him or return his phone calls unless Ravi signed a written consent. Eventually, the family physician responded to the family's request to refer Ravi to an Indian psychiatrist, preferably Hindu and familiar with the culture.

At the initial evaluation, the Asian-Indian psychiatrist learned that Ravi had been born in India and had moved to New York with his parents and older sister when he was a year old. A younger sister was born in the U.S. His father had graduated with a medical degree, and his mother had a bachelor's degree in Biology from India. Upon moving to the United States (U.S.), his father obtained a job as an aide in a radiology office and his mother remained a homemaker. The father worked full-time and used the local library to prepare for his qualifying exams. Over the course of several years, he passed his exams, but due to low scores and multiple attempts, he failed to obtain a residency. After six years, he gave up on becoming a practicing physician in the U.S. and instead focused on business. He purchased a franchise fast food restaurant. He did well in his business, stock market portfolio, and real estate investments. When the children were in school, his wife was able to assist him in his ventures and oversee the back-office functions. Both parents were observant Hindus and attended the Hindu temple frequently with their children. At home, they prayed twice a day, and the children participated in their prayers and Poojas.

Ravi was a full-term, normal delivery. His milestones were normal and his development uneventful. He did well in school. Academics came easy for him, and he did not have to put in the effort to excel. He was somewhat shy and was not interested in sports. He had a few good friends. He spent a significant amount of time on the computer and playing videos games. He often made extra money fixing the computers of his parent's friends. Following high school, he went to college and obtained a degree in computer science. He worked as a programmer in a well-known company. He was well respected and had been promoted twice in the last 3 years. He insisted that his symptoms had not affected his performance at work. Ravi had no significant medical or substance abuse history. He lived alone in a one-bedroom apartment. His parents and younger sister lived in a home a mile away.

Family history of known psychiatric illness was denied. However, on persistent questioning, the mother revealed that there were two close relatives on the father's side who were considered "different". An uncle spent his adult life writing mantras 108 times each day. This progressed to spending the major portion of the day writing and praying. There was significant distress in the family because he refused to discard his notebooks. Another uncle was a reclusive individual who had no friends. He tended to go on long walks and often observed Maunam (vows of silence) for one day a week.

Diagnostic Formulation

Ravi presented with onset of intrusive thoughts that were distressing, as well as specific rituals with the intent of alleviating the anxiety emanating from those thoughts. There was no evidence of hallucinations, delusions, or disorganized thought. There was no evidence of sustained changes in mood. While some of his symptoms were around issues of food, the onset and course did not justify consideration of an eating disorder. Ravi denied any use of alcohol or illicit drugs. Based on this clinical history, he was diagnosed to have Obsessive Compulsive Disorder (OCD).

In order for treatment to be optimal and successful, the cultural aspects, especially the symbolic meanings at each stage of life, needed to be explored and addressed proactively. In treating teenagers born and raised in the U.S., it is important to review areas of inter-generational conflict, including choices of clothing, curfew, and dating. Ravi had not dated anyone as his parents wanted him to get married in an arranged marriage. In addition to stage of life, it is important to explore issues around diet. With South Asians, dietary preferences are only occasionally about health choices. They represent strongly held religious views. Ravi was a strict vegetarian like his family.

It is also important to explore religious rituals and symbols. Ravi grew up with family who held religious beliefs and practices. He visited temples every week. He was very familiar with the religious practices himself. These included chanting prayers, puja, and practices around fasting.

In treating South Asian patients, it is imperative that the clinician take detailed religious history of the family, as well as the individual. It is difficult to call traditional and culturally syntonic religious practices pathological until it is clear that such practices interfere in the person's daily functioning and relationships. As noticed by Ravi's parents, his thoughts lead to repeated compulsions. The clinician recognized that the obsessive-compulsive behavior helped Ravi to contain the anxiety. His behavior gradually started to interfere in his daily life.

Management

During the first several sessions, the major goal was to establish a therapeutic relationship. Ravi related well to a less formal style and was pleased with some commonalties. At the request of Ravi, the psychiatrist made a few personal disclosures (e.g., school attended, educational background) in a non-defensive manner. The personal questions stopped after the first few sessions. Another challenge was dealing with questions from Ravi's parents. Initially Ravi did not want his parents to receive any information other than what he chose to share with them. Later, he agreed to his parents sitting in for the last few minutes of a session with the psychiatrist only responding to very general questions, such as the benefit of talk therapy or the indications and risks associated with psychiatric medications.

Ravi felt comfortable by the middle of his second session. He became relatively open about his symptoms. He was intelligent, articulate, and often displayed humor. However, he was defensive and closed when discussing relationships. The psychiatrist explored several issues, but did not push any specific issue.

In the third session, the psychiatrist discussed the diagnosis of OCD with Ravi. Ravi said that he knew it all along, even though he had never discussed it with anyone else. He agreed to a family session, which was attended by his parents and older sister. The psychiatrist educated them about Ravi's illness and its manifestations. The father was initially insulted to consider a psychiatric diagnosis and the possibility that there might be a family history, but later was relieved that Ravi's behavior had a name. The psychiatrist suggested a treatment plan consisting of psychotherapy and medication. Initially, there was objection from his mother who felt the medication could be addictive. She had known of people becoming 'zombies' on psychiatric medicines. Ravi's sister advocated for medications. Ravi was ambivalent and wondered if there was scientific proof about causation and treatment of OCD. Later, after discussion within the family, reading about OCD, and consulting their family physician, both Ravi and family agreed to medications. He was started on an antidepressant and the dose was gradually increased. Ravi's symptoms responded well. He experienced a rapid abatement of his obsessions and compulsions. He also felt much calmer and had no more angry outbursts.

After 12 sessions, Ravi opened up about his sexuality stating that he had known he was gay from the time he was 10 years of age. He had not shared this secret with anyone and wanted it kept strictly confidential. Over the years, he had a rich fantasy life, but had not acted on his homosexual urges. In the Fall of 2015, he had had his first sexual encounter with a man he met in a bar. He enjoyed the experience, but was also markedly anxious. Following the encounter, he was convinced that he had sinned and would be punished. The feelings worsened over the next few weeks. He began to feel dirty and needed to wash and shower frequently. He felt that his actions would cause harm to his parents and other relatives. He devised rituals that would prevent this from happening. He confided that many of the arguments he had with his parents during the TV coverage of the 2016 presidential elections were triggered by the mention of gay marriage by politicians or political pundits.

Ravi felt some relief from the catharsis. However, he continued to feel guilty. In subsequent sessions, the focus was on normalizing his homosexuality. During this stage of therapy, there were many references to sin and religion, which needed exploration and reframing. By session 20, the psychiatrist explored the idea of 'coming out'. With some reluctance, he agreed to inform his immediate family, but wanted the psychiatrist to be present. A family session was arranged with all immediate family. Following initial avoidance, Ravi did inform them he was gay. His mother began sobbing and wailing loudly. She spoke of the specific girl she wanted him to meet and the wedding she had planned for her only son. Ravi's father was cold, and after initially being silent and displaying no emotion said, "Well I am sure the doctor knows how to treat this. It must be curable". He then got up and walked out. However, both sisters and his brother-in-law were physically and emotionally warm and conveyed their commitment to accept and love him regardless. Both sisters were surprised and hurt that he had not confided in them earlier.

Following this session, there was rapid improvement. Ravi felt energized. He made a list of his inner circle, met with each person individually, and disclosed that he was gay. He was pleasantly surprised that, other than an aunt who lived in Canada, everyone accepted him. As his symptoms receded, the psychiatrist was able to lower the dose of the medication to a maintenance dose, which Ravi accepted. As time went on, his relationship with his father improved. Their arguments about politics, especially around marriage equality and immigration, continued, but with more humor and acceptance of the opposing point of view. His father was able to take the stance that while he did not think homosexuality was normal, he loved this son enough that he would support him. Ravi's mother was less accepting and took the stance that he was going through a phase and that he would change when "he met the right girl."

Summary

Ravi is a 25-year-old single Asian-Indian male working as a computer programmer who was diagnosed with OCD. A confounding factor was hiding his homosexuality from those around him. His case illustrates the intersection of biological vulnerability and stress from cultural and intrapsychic conflict resulting in symptomatology disruptive to him and his family. Culturally sensitive psychotherapy with targeted psychopharmacology were effective interventions.

Teaching Points

1. Establishing rapport and forming a therapeutic relationship is a critical first step in treatment. It becomes particularly important when cultural and religious sensitivities are in play. Being knowledgeable is always an advantage, but in the absence of knowledge, being open to learning with a non-judgmental stance is helpful.
2. South Asian families are not a homogenous group. There are wide differences in socioeconomic and educational stratification. Psychological mindedness and acceptance of psychiatric conditions

also fall across a wide spectrum. Similarly, the entire range of defenses from intellectualization to denial are often in vivid display. The initial assessment needs to include an evaluation of these factors.

3. A frequent sub-cultural issue that manifests itself is the resistance to the 'professional stance.' South Asians often make a demand for informality. It takes tact in maintaining boundaries without being insulting or rejecting. Being warm and friendly is a tricky proposition with South Asian patients (and others). When the exploration (What made you ask that?) of the underlying intent of an assertion or question meets with resistance, it needs to be explained and often has to be reframed.

4. Another issue that faces a therapist treating a South Asian patient is the conflict between individual autonomy and collectivist society. The therapist is constantly dealing with the therapeutic aspirational goal of reducing distress for the individual and what the group (such as the family unit) can handle or permit.

5. The interface between religious issues and psychiatric symptoms need to be handled with care. This can take many forms. The normal practice of Hindu religion often involves rituals. When one grows up with these, they are seen as normative, even when excessive. In fact, in certain situations it could confer greater respect and prestige. It is challenging to draw the distinction between pathology and an exaggerated norm.

Rahim: Unclear Mental Illness in the Setting of Inconsistent Follow-up

Case History

Rahim, a 23-year-old single male of South Asian descent, sought outpatient care at a local mental health clinic following involuntary admission to an inpatient psychiatry unit for agitation and threatening behaviors directed towards his family. He was to receive case management services and medication management.

Rahim was born in a small village in northern India. No perinatal problems were reported. Developmental milestones were reported as being within normal limits. His parents immigrated to the United States (U.S.) when he was just 18 months old. His parents struggled financially and had to make multiple moves within the U. S. with hopes of better opportunities.

Rahim was the oldest of three, with a teenage sister in high school and a brother in elementary school. His siblings were reportedly well adjusted and doing well in school. Rahim had been having emotional problems since age twelve. While in middle school, he had displayed intermittent bouts of aggression and oppositional behaviors. Rahim was frequently bullied in school. He would not elaborate much on this, but it was thought related to him dressing with a headpiece in accordance with his Muslim faith. He did not feel the need to tell this to his parents. He coped with the bullying by either skipping school or fighting back, resulting in suspensions from school. His parents were surprised by reports of his truancy and fights with peers. Because of his behavioral issues, he was transferred to a school that dealt with children who had behavioral issues. His mother was annoyed by his behavior, ashamed of his temper, and frustrated about her unsuccessful attempts to discipline him. Rahim's parents would compare his "immature and irresponsible behavior" to his younger siblings who were doing well socially and academically. This in turn frustrated Rahim, and he would then verbally attack his parents and siblings. Some of these outbursts were triggered by interactions with his parents and siblings, and sometimes there were no clear triggers. Examples of severe episodes included breaking the windows of the family car and making death threats to his brother.

Two anger outbursts at school and a third at home led to a string of psychiatric hospitalizations. The hospital discharges were followed by his parents sending him to India to stay with his maternal grandparents in a village home, so that he could get "supervision from grandparents, fresh air, and have less chance of getting into trouble." This also seemed an easier solution to them, as they continued to struggle financially. He would stay there for a few weeks to months at a time and receive brief, psychiatric treatment while in India. It is unclear if he had behavioral outbursts in India and if they led to hospitalization.

Rahim's last hospitalization in the U.S., the one prior to seeking outpatient treatment at the local mental health clinic, was an involuntary admission for violent behavior. The request for involuntary psychiatric admission was secondary to homicidal threats towards his father. At the time of assessment, he was noted to be agitated, threatening to kill his father for abusing him, and having never loved him. At the hospital, he was treated with antipsychotics and experienced good improvement in all of his symptoms. He was discharged with the diagnosis of Schizoaffective Disorder, Bipolar Type, and was placed on a long-acting antipsychotic injection. This decision was based on poor adherence with oral medications. His parents complied with the treatment team's recommendation to follow-up at an outpatient mental health clinic, choosing to continue treatment in the U.S. instead of again sending him to India.

The psychiatrist who did the initial evaluation in the outpatient facility noted that there were huge gaps in his social and developmental history as the parents had great difficulty providing the history. On review of the records from his psychiatric hospitalization, it was noted that Rahim struggled academically in school and quit after the 9th grade. His work history was sparse with difficulty maintaining simple jobs. He had been fired at least once for poor attendance. There was no history of drug or alcohol use. His medical history was significant for essential hypertension, chronic kidney disease, and hyperlipidemia. There was no family history of psychiatric illness. Rahim was given multiple diagnoses, including bipolar disorder, schizophrenia, and schizoaffective disorder.

During his outpatient care, Rahim's family was closely involved in his treatment. His mother accompanied him on his monthly visits. During this time, he received the antipsychotic injection and had sessions with either the psychiatrist, case manager, or both. His psychiatrist was of Indian origin and could speak his native language. The evaluation / interviews were always conducted in Rahim's native language by the psychiatrist, as both Rahim and his mother were not fluent in English. On each of these visits, Rahim presented as a quiet, respectful young man.

The visits with the psychiatrist were designed primarily for medication management. The sessions with the case manager focused on addressing psychosocial issues raised, such as insurance issues, making appointments with primary care provider, housing, and school / job situations. However, there were times when the patient and his mother felt they needed more time with the psychiatrist to discuss issues that they could not communicate well with the case manager secondary to a language barrier. There were a few episodes of miscommunication with the case manager. One example included the case manager referring the patient to a primary care provider for management of hypertension and chronic kidney disease. Rahim, however, misunderstood this as referral to another psychiatrist and chose not to follow-up. This and other situations resolved quickly after the patient / mother discussed them with the psychiatrist. The psychiatrist would have combined sessions with the case manager and help resolve the misunderstandings.

Diagnostic Formulation

Rahim has carried various psychiatric diagnoses and the true underlying diagnosis is still not clear. It is unclear if the frequent aggressive outbursts that Rahim had in his childhood were unhealthy coping mechanisms associated with the taunting and bullying or paranoia to real and perceived bullying. In addition to the complexity of his illness, a major factor associated with the challenge of making a diagnosis was the frequent trips he made to India during either an exacerbation or following a hospitalization, which resulted in inconsistent psychiatric care. His parents hoped that by sending Rahm back home to his grandparents in the village, he would grow out of the disruptive behaviors. No details were available on what happened in India, but when his mood and behavior stabilized; his parents would have him sent back. Rahim came from a rural background, of modest means and a patriarchal society, with increased expectations due to him being the eldest child and the first-born son of his parents. His parents were not highly educated and came from a farming community that takes pride in hard work and not relying on handouts. Immigration to the U.S. was not the ticket to financial freedom they had hoped. Rahim's parents had limited time, money, and resources, which led to inconsistency and irregularity of follow-up visits and interfered with establishment of a proper diagnosis and treatment. Neither Rahim, nor his family, fit the mold of the "successful minority", the group that immigrates with college degrees and English language fluency. If it were not for the school system calling Rahim's behavioral problems to attention, establishment of mental health care may have been further delayed.

Management

Management of Rahim's symptoms included a team approach with the psychiatrist and the case manager complementing each other. The psychiatrist focused on medication management and provided supportive therapy and psychoeducation. The case manager addressed psychosocial stressors raised by the patient and his parents, such as insurance issues, appointments with primary care provider, housing, and school / job situations. She also introduced appropriate community resources and linked the patient and family to appropriate entitlement programs, all of which were helpful. When Rahim or his parents had questions about their discussions with the case manager or needed clarifications, they would re-discuss them with the psychiatrist, who would help resolve the miscommunications jointly with the case manager. Thus, follow-up visits with the psychiatrist were used not only for illness education and medication management, but also supportive and family therapy interventions. This kind of teamwork allowed Rahim to obtain health insurance, which greatly helped in compliance with medications and consistent follow-up.

Overall, this multipronged approach greatly helped Rahim and his parents. Rahim's mood and behavior stabilized. His parents are hopeful that he will be able to obtain and maintain a job, get married, and live independently. He continues to be compliant with medications and psychiatric follow-up. His parents also accompany him intermittently.

In the part of the U.S. where Rahim lives, both he and his family are in the minority, as regarded by both the South Asian community and the mainstream community. The staff at the mental health clinic were ill prepared to deal with this group, expecting them to be educated and well off like all the other Indian Americans in the area they had contact with. The South Asian community often socializes within its own ranks. Families like Rahim's do not move in those same circles and are yet seen, by the mainstream culture, as part of the same model minority. As a result, those that are still struggling end up not having the needed expertise or networks with medical professionals or community resources. The stigma, lack of awareness and denial of mental health issues, and the "keeping up of appearances" all lead to challenges in access to, and utilization of, mental health care.

Summary

Rahim is a 23-year-old single South Asian male who immigrated to the U.S. with his parents at a very young age and carries an unclear psychiatric diagnosis with symptoms of agitation and threatening behaviors. He is the first born of his parents with no known familial risk factors for mental illness or any other chronic illness. There is no history of substance abuse. He had early onset psychiatric illness and has most recently been formulated as having Schizoaffective Disorder, Bipolar Type, even though the diagnosis is still in question. The repeated bullying in school, multiple moves within the country, and frequent travels to India interfered with establishing the diagnosis and obtaining consistent psychiatric care. The recent establishment of outpatient psychiatric care, with a team-based approach to help Rahim and his parents navigate the complex health system, has greatly helped in fostering therapeutic relationships that have led to successful treatment outcomes.

Teaching Points

1. Not all South Asians have made a successful transition to a higher social class on immigration to the U.S. South Asians are just as likely to be underinsured or uninsured.
2. Stress of immigration may lead to major mental illness, in vulnerable folks, in the absence of any known history of mental illness.
3. A treating psychiatrist may have to do more than just prescribe medications. Going the extra mile and connecting the patient / family to a case manager and other community resources can help in improving quality of life and reducing stress and caregiver burden.
4. Psychiatrists well versed in the patient's culture may have to educate other clinicians.
5. Educating a family dealing with mental illness should be done on an ongoing basis as the comprehension of a chronic mental illness may not be easily grasped or accepted.

Mohan: A Different Husband, Father, and Businessman Following Traumatic Brain Injury

Case History

Mohan, a 48-year-old married male who was born, raised in India, and immigrated to the United States (U.S.) in his early 30s, was evaluated for change in behavior and mood after a motor vehicle accident. His birth, early development, and childhood were normal in all respects. He excelled throughout his education and graduated with a Ph.D. in computer science from a prestigious institute in India. After immigrating to the U.S., he worked as a computer programmer in a well-known organization for a few years and then left to start his own software company. It was a struggle at first, but the company gradually grew and over the years became very successful, with Mohan serving as the Chief Executive Officer (CEO). He had been happily married for 20 years. He had two teenage daughters that were in high school and doing well. He had no history of alcohol or other illicit substance abuse. His medical history was significant only for hypertension. There was no history of psychiatric illness in his family. He had no personal history of previous psychiatric illness.

About two years prior to evaluation, he was involved in a motor vehicle accident. Computerized tomography scan of the head revealed multiple contusions in the frontal and temporal regions of the brain and a left subarachnoid hemorrhage, which required immediate drainage. He regained consciousness about an hour after admission to the trauma care unit. He did not sustain any other bodily injuries. After three days in the neurosurgical intensive care unit, he was transferred to the medical floor for blood pressure stabilization. He remained on the medical floor for one week. From the floor, he was discharged to home and began an outpatient neurorehabilitation program, where he received twelve weeks of occupational and speech/language therapy.

After discharge from the hospital, his wife noticed a change in his mood and behavior. He was quick to anger, became easily frustrated, needed frequent reminders, and had difficulty planning. Once considered thoughtful, considerate, and organized, he was now forgetful, rude, and disorganized. About three months after the accident, he went back to work. Unfortunately, organizational and interpersonal skills, which once came easily to him, were now difficult. He would forget meetings and become irate when reminded. During the meetings he did attend, he was no longer diplomatic, but impolite and abrupt. The breaking point came when he impulsively and unilaterally invested company money in a stock which collapsed, costing his firm about 2 million dollars. The board of directors requested that he step down, which he did with great reluctance.

In the following months, his wife noticed that he was dull and tired, uninterested in playing his usual game of tennis or exercising, and emotionally withdrawn from family and friends. His sleep was poor, and a reduced appetite led to a weight loss of 10 pounds. Contrary to reality, he had firm beliefs that he was going bankrupt and that only the financial compensation from his death would save them. His grooming and appearance declined. He had difficulty concentrating and reading. His wife noticed that he would become extremely angry easily. His children hesitated to consult with him about their problems and instead approached their mother. After her family medical leave ended, his wife resumed working as a teacher. Mohan would get angry when she worked late and accuse her of not caring for him anymore because he was "useless." In response to requests from his wife to see a doctor, he would often say that no one could help him as this was his karma or a curse on the family. He told his wife that he was in pain. He described the pain as a sensation of pressure and heaviness running from the top of his head to the bottom of his feet, "his whole body." He reported nausea and a sense of fullness as the cause of his poor appetite. His wife was worried about his dullness and body pain, but did not push treatment as she was concerned of the negative impact doing so may have on their family. She felt it was important to manage family issues within the family and not involve others.

Mohan's wife came home one day to find him lying on the bed unconscious near an empty Tylenol bottle. He left a note stating that his death would end the curse on the family and pave the way for his children's bright future. She called 911 and the paramedics rushed him to the hospital. After medical stabilization, Mohan was transferred to a psychiatric facility. At first, he was not happy on the unit and refused to give permission for the treatment team to talk to his family. He was started on a low dose of a selective serotonin reuptake inhibitor, which he took reluctantly at first. Later, his compliance improved. His antidepressant dose was gradually increased. The treatment team explained his illness and treatment using biological terms. He responded well to terms such as "brain injury" and "neurochemical imbalance". His mood gradually improved, he agreed to have family meetings, and he began to participate in group therapy. At first, he shared minimally for fear that his disclosures may leak out to his coworkers and other members of his community, but later became active as the benefits of group therapy were discussed and the rules of confidentiality emphasized. He was very excited and participated fully when his treatment team asked him to lead sessions on meditation and yoga.

He was later discharged to an outpatient program with recommendations to be followed closely by a psychiatrist and a cognitive behavioral therapist. He was compliant with medication, but was ambivalent about outpatient therapy. He did not believe psychotherapy would be an avenue to get his job back or change his karma. His compliance with therapy gradually improved, and he began to look forward to his therapy appointments. He called his therapist by various names, including "guru," "guide," and "best friend." He even invited his therapist to his daughter's graduation party. He was upset when the invitation was declined, and the therapist spent a couple of sessions reinforcing the importance of professional boundaries. After a year of outpatient treatment, Mohan reported feeling about 80% of baseline. His wife and children also noticed improvement. Mohan continues in monthly outpatient treatment and even brings his wife to sessions every few months.

Diagnostic Formulation

Mohan experienced an acquired, rather than idiopathic, psychiatric syndrome. The biological contribution to his clinical presentation was trauma to the frontotemporal region of the brain, which increases the risk for depression and executive functioning deficits. These changes were evident in his new onset disorganization, impulsivity, disinhibition, and inability to regulate emotions and behavior. These changes contributed to Mohan losing his position of CEO at the company he founded. Psychologically, this left a previously confident, social, emotionally intelligent individual feeling demoralized, hopeless and "useless." He lost the structure and routine of his day. At home, his children no longer sought him out for advice, instead turning to their mother. Together, these feelings and losses may have worsened the biological depression, which often follows frontal lobe damage after traumatic brain injury (TBI). The interaction of the above biological and psychological factors with social stressors, such as the decrease in family income after his job loss and the change in family dynamics after his injury, can all be considered as etiological factors in the development and maintenance of his mood disorder.

Culturally, Mohan had great difficulty accepting the contributions of the above factors to the changes he experienced, instead explaining them in terms of karma, a curse on the family, and the natural reason to be sad because of his job loss. He did not use the terms sad or depressed. Instead, he and his family used words such as dull or body pain to describe his feelings. Stigma of what others will think seemed to prevent Mohan, as well as his wife, from seeking and accepting the help he needed. Unable to ask for help, he spiraled downwards and finally attempted suicide. As such, this cultural aspect contributed to the delay in help seeking.

Even though the changes experienced by Mohan could leave anyone feeling demoralized, it can strike an especially strong blow to the ego of an Indian male, as traditional Indian society is patriarchal. Men are regarded as the "CEO" of the house – the main breadwinners and the decision makers. The view is that the husband makes the rules and will do everything in his power to maintain the family. Loss of this role can be a blow to the male ego, which can manifest as anger, irritability, and paranoia and, in extreme cases, even violence.

Somatization of psychiatric problems is quite common among South Asians who avoid use of terms such as depression due to stigma and concern that such a diagnosis is a sign of weakness, failure, or an unwillingness to strive. Psychiatric problems are often expressed as physical symptoms; most commonly headaches, backache, nausea, dizziness, and fatigue. In contrast to the Western model of directly expressing emotions, the South Asians prefer a holistic model of integrating emotional and physical symptoms and expressing emotional distress through one's body. In addition, South Asians are group-oriented, family-oriented, allocentric unlike the Western culture, which is idiocentric. Expression of negative emotions is considered disruptive to the group / family harmony and many choose to bottle their feelings and say nothing or channel their emotional symptoms into physical symptoms, which are more acceptable.

Discussing problematic issues outside the family is neither encouraged nor respected. Silence is valued over the disclosure of family secrets. Because of the importance of maintaining secrets within the family, neither Mohan nor his wife had reached out to others for assistance. Networking, sharing information, and forming support groups are valued in the Western culture and considered therapeutic. However, this may not be an option to Indians who value stoicism, non-disclosure, and a conservative orientation. In addition, borrowing or obtaining loans is a foreign concept for many Indians, as traditionally they are raised to spend only what they have. With the loss of his CEO position, there was a significant drop in Mohan's finances. This caused a lot of stress for him leading to delusional thinking (e.g., going bankrupt, financial compensation from his death would save family) an important precipitating factor for his suicide attempt.
]

Management

Like with any patient-clinician relationship, establishing rapport is the cornerstone of successful treatment. The key ingredients for building strong rapport include clinician characteristics, such as being honest, non-judgmental, respecting the patients' values and beliefs, and accepting the patient holistically for who they are. The therapeutic relationship with

Mohan greatly improved when the treatment team was able to identify and make use of one of Mohan's strengths. He felt valued and supported after he was asked to take the lead on non-Western therapeutic strategies, such as yoga and meditation.

Acceptance of emotional problems as an illness does not come very easily to Indian patients, as evidenced by Mohan's unhappiness to be admitted to a facility for treatment of emotional problems. Many are reluctant to seek treatment because of beliefs that medications or therapy can do little to change these situations. In addition, reluctance is also secondary to stigma, shame, and embarrassment. They feel ashamed of their weakness and embarrassed to seek treatment for a problem they should have easily overcome. These concerns are often deep rooted in the Asian-Indian culture. Providing education about mental illness in an honest, non-judgmental way abates stigma and shame. Repeated education using analogies of medical illness (e.g., hypertension, diabetes), drawing cartoons of the brain / brain chemicals, or wherever possible using examples from Indian epics (e.g. Ramayana, Mahabarth), can help. It is important to stress that mental illnesses are real health problems, which can improve with treatment.

Mohan's treatment was comprehensive and included pharmacotherapy (biological treatment) and psychotherapy (to help him cope with his psychosocial stressors). Mohan was at first not interested in therapy, calling it a waste of time. His treatment team patiently educated him about treatment strategies and the importance of approaching his problem from different angles. Most importantly, they paid attention to his complaints, responded sensitively to his questions, used therapy time to learn about Mohan's cultural values, and even have him take over some sessions, when they felt it was appropriate.

When prescribing medications, the treatment team was cognizant of the fact that there are limited research studies on pharmacokinetics and pharmacodynamics of psychotropics in the Asian-Indian population. They discussed this with Mohan and emphasized the importance of regular follow-up and close monitoring. The medication was started at the lowest dose and the dose gradually increased to clinically therapeutic levels. It was explained to Mohan that a pill would not fix him and that he had to do his part to get better (i.e. participate in individual and group therapy).

Many South Asians equate sacrifice to love; giving up something for the good of the family is honored and valued. Mohan's suicide attempt was an act of sacrifice to benefit his family. South Asians also do not consider death final. They believe in re-birth and in reincarnation. The soul is immortal and after death transferred to another human or species. These values help in conceptualizing death as not the end, but a passing on. Therapy sessions focused on discussions of sacrifice, its pros and cons, and the importance of channeling feelings of love and sacrifice into productive and healthy behaviors. As Mohan engaged more in therapy, he gradually began to look at his therapist as his best friend and advisor. He expected his therapist to give him concrete directions. This is not uncommon among South Asians. They expect the psychiatrist / therapist to be proactive and provide concrete advice. Authority figures are held in high regard and greatly respected. South Asian patients may even find it difficult to voice their feelings or even ask for an explanation. Not accepting personal invitations can be considered as a rejection. Not making direct eye contact, weak handshake, and maintaining distance are all expressions of respect for authority figures, and clinicians should be careful about misinterpreting them as residual symptoms of depression. Sometimes, clinicians need to take an authoritarian role and provide guidance. Group therapy sessions can also be challenging as South Asians find it concerning to share problems with others and disclose private feelings. The concerns are not only about confidentiality and leaking of information, but because restraint is valued over free-expression and autonomy. It took several sessions before Mohan participated actively in group therapy and he was more compliant when sessions included yoga and meditation rather than interactive talk sessions.

Lastly, Mohan accepted the DSM-5 diagnosis 'Neurocognitive Disorder secondary to TBI.' This diagnostic term had all the words that appealed to him: neuro, cognitive, and TBI. Clinicians can also do this by taking a symptomatic approach and focusing on symptoms such as insomnia, fatigue, or loss of appetite. If a patient or family is finding it difficult to accept diagnostic terms (e.g., major depression), it is acceptable to call it by another name.

Summary

Mohan is a 48-year-old married male of South Asian descent who was evaluated for change in behavior and mood after a motor vehicle accident. After evaluation, it was determined that he had developed major depression after the injury and he struggled with this diagnosis for a period of time without obtaining any help. A suicide attempt brought him to the hospital and later into psychiatric treatment. Reluctant at first to engage in treatment, he gradually came around as his treatment team patiently and respectfully worked with him providing comprehensive pharmacological and psychological treatment while being sensitive to his cultural values.

Teaching Points

1. Patients with major depression may not always report sadness, unhappiness, or low mood. They may present with chronic physical symptoms. It is important to ask closed-ended questions about mood symptoms if major depression is suspected.
2. Successful treatment is based on establishing rapport. Sometimes clinicians need to think outside the box and consider specific ways to connect with an individual patient.
3. Authority figures are respected and can be considered gurus, advisors, or even close friends. It is important to establish professional boundaries at the start of treatment. A weak handshake, poor eye contact, and low voice are not always signs of depression, and may be signs of respect for the clinician.
4. Psychiatric diagnostic terms are often misunderstood. There is no need to pressure patients to accept a diagnosis. Treatment should be problem-oriented and symptom-focused.
5. The treatment team was cognizant of the fact that there are limited research studies on pharmacokinetics and pharmacodynamics of psychotropics in the Asian-Indian population.

Amar: New Onset Psychosis In an Elderly Man with Brain Tumor

Case History

Amar, a 73-year-old married male of Indian descent, was referred to outpatient neuropsychiatric care in the setting of late-life behavioral changes. After a thorough assessment and work-up, he was diagnosed with a brain tumor.

Amar was born in a medium-sized town in northern India. No perinatal problems were reported. Developmental milestones were reported as being within normal limits. He did not have a known past psychiatric history. He denied any family history of psychiatric illness, though he did admit that these things were not discussed in his family. Amar was the oldest of three siblings, and he was very close to his family. He was retired from a government job. At time of initial assessment, he had been married for 51 years, and he had a close and supportive marriage with his wife. He had two sons, one lived in India and the other in the United States (U.S.). He and his wife split their time between India and the U.S.

At the age of 73, Amar developed subacute onset of paranoia, something he had never experienced before. He felt that his neighbors were spying on him and his family, and that they meant him harm. He reported hearing whispers from other houses. He stayed awake as much as he could to protect his family from these intruders. After these symptoms developed, his family took him to the local ED, where he had a computerized tomography (CT) scan. On CT, there was evidence of a tumor in the right hemisphere. Further workup with magnetic resonance imaging (MRI) confirmed a right frontotemporal tumor. Surgical resection was completed, and the biopsy revealed a Grade II astrocytoma. He had radiation and chemotherapy over the next year. In addition, an antipsychotic was prescribed, and he experienced complete resolution of psychotic symptoms. During his course of treatment, he stayed in the United States, and his wife continued to split her time between India and the United States.

After it was deemed medically safe for him to travel, he went on a trip to India. It was during this trip that he experienced the first of several recurrences of psychosis. During that trip, he stopped his antipsychotic as he did not want to be on a medication for "crazy people." Both sons, along with his wife, encouraged Amar to stop taking the antipsychotic despite his doctor's recommendations to the contrary. His psychotic symptoms quickly resurfaced, and a physician in India put him back on the same medication, which again resulted in full resolution of his psychotic symptoms. Shortly after, he and his wife returned to the U.S. at which time repeat brain imaging revealed no new tumor growth. He and his family interpreted the psychotic episode as being caused by getting overwhelmed with visiting relatives in India and a lack of sleep. After a few months, Amar and his family again decided, against the doctor's recommendation, to stop the antipsychotic.

Unfortunately, he again had recurrence of psychotic symptoms, with prominent delusional thinking and auditory hallucinations. Again, he was placed on the same medicine by his doctor, and again he got better. This pattern continued as his family insisted that he get off the medication once stabilized. He and his family felt that he could manage his symptoms by stress management techniques, particularly meditation and yoga. Amar was always into meditation and yoga, and he found that these practices really helped keep him calm and centered.

Despite him regularly doing meditation and yoga, when he was not taking an antipychotic medication, he would develop psychotic symptoms. Brain imaging during these recurrences consistently showed no new tumor growth. He was no longer traveling to India as he associated trips with recurrence of symptoms. His son in the U.S. was not in favor of him restarting his medication, though his daughter-in-law (who was born in the U.S., but was of Indian descent) felt strongly that he should not risk decompensation. Eventually, based on his doctor's continued insistence, he consistently took an antipsychotic medication even after stabilization. His family did not relent with their requests for the medication to be discontinued. The family felt he was fine, and they felt that psychotropic medications should only be taken for short periods of time (like antibiotics). His physician, based on the family and patient's continued insistence, lowered the dose of the antipsychotic. Amar did not decompensate over the span of the next year despite being on just a low dose.

Diagnostic Formulation

Amar likely had psychosis secondary to a general medical condition (in this case, his brain tumor). The location of his brain tumor (right frontotemporal lobe) is consistent with the onset of psychotic symptoms. It is thought that psychosis can occur with the combination of decreased frontal lobe control along with disruption of temporal lobe cortical and subcortical circuits. Lesions in the right hemisphere may be more likely to cause psychotic symptoms than left hemisphere lesions. An interesting component of this case is that Amar had psychotic relapses even without evident tumor regrowth. This may suggest that he had a genetic vulnerability to psychosis with the brain lesion causing a tipping point. In addition to the complexity of his illness, a major risk factor leading to decompensation was the frequent trips he made to India, which resulted in inconsistent psychiatric care. These kinds of trips are common among South Asians, and may reflect the fact that globalization has led to dispersal of family across the world. These trips may also serve to maintain relations with extended family, maintain social responsibilities in India, try alternative systems of medicine (e.g., Ayurveda), or be in more familiar surroundings. Amar did not try Ayurvedic or herbal formulations while in India, but he did do meditation and yoga more regularly.

Lack of understanding about neuropsychiatric symptoms / mental illness, despite globalization, is still prevalent. Psychiatric symptoms may be viewed as secondary to lifestyle issues, such as poor sleep or stress, as opposed to being biologically-based. Often symptoms are a result of a combination of these factors. In this case, even though Amar had a clear biological basis of his psychosis (his brain tumor), shame and embarrassment of having a family member taking "crazy medications," and the strength of the belief that lifestyle changes alone can treat psychosis, led to his repeated decompensations.

Management

Psychiatric management of Amar in the U.S. was done at a specialty neuropsychiatry clinic at a major academic medical center. His care was collaborative with the neuropsychiatrist embedded in the neuro-oncology service. Despite the medical setting, and the clear connection between his symptoms and his brain lesion, the stigma of taking an antipsychotic was clearly prominent. This compounded the challenges of dealing with a complicated illness. Stigma is, unfortunately, quite universal regarding mental illness. This is certainly the case with South Asians, arguably even more so than typical Westerners. The question not often addressed is: "Why is there such a universal stigma of mental illness? Why not such stigma of heart disease, pulmonary disease, or liver disease? What is special about mental illness to bring about such strong stigma?"

One could argue that the answer to this question gets to the heart of the human condition and subsequent perennial and deep philosophical questions. We, as humans, identify our "selves" with our brain, not our heart, lungs, liver, or any other organ. If the brain is our "self," then it is logical to feel that we should be able to control our brain. In Indian culture, the notion of *Maya,* that reality is an illusion, and the notion of *Karma,* the idea that some things are meant to happen to us, that free will is not completely free, impact views of mental illness. In Amar's case, given that he was into Indian philosophy and meditation and yoga, leveraging Indian philosophical ideas helped to get his buy-in into taking medication. With Amar, the psychiatrist could make the argument that just like one would treat a heart, lung, or liver condition, one should treat a brain condition. The psychiatrist explained that psychosis was a result of damage to the brain, not a result of damage to the "self." It was explained to Amar that damage to his brain was the cause of symptoms and therefore he should not feel defensive, just as one would not feel defensive about consequences of a heart, lung, or liver condition. This stance helped Amar in accepting medication (albeit at a low dose).

Stress management techniques like yoga and meditation were incorporated into the treatment plan for this patient, with the idea that perhaps while we cannot be fully responsible for what happens to us, we can be responsible for how we react to it. Yoga and meditation may help in managing one's reactions. Though this was not done in this particular case, depending on the level of philosophical interest in the patient, one could even discuss how there may be an element of *Karma* which is unchangeable (*Prarabhda Karma*), and an element that is changeable (*Sanchit Karma*).

Summary

Amar is a 73-year-old married male of Indian descent who developed psychotic symptoms in the setting of a right frontotemporal brain tumor. He responded well to oncological and psychiatric treatment, with resolution of his psychotic symptoms. Unfortunately, the cultural stigma of mental illness symptoms prevented him from continuing on his medications. Both he and his family insisted on stopping the antipsychotic, despite the physician's clear recommendation. Repeated decompensations occurred until he is now stable with a low dose of antipsychotic. Going forward, there is still a risk that he will stop his medication, but leveraging Indian philosophical concepts of *Maya* and *Karma* was one way to use his cultural milieu to help with treatment.

Teaching Points

1. It is not uncommon for South Asians to seek psychiatric treatment only in times of crises. When they do, symptoms are often severe requiring urgent medical evaluation and treatment.
2. Stigma about mental illness can be so strong that even when there is a clear biological basis of the symptoms, patients still may not want treatment.

3. Stigma about mental illness is universal, perhaps because of the sense that we all have complete free will and that psychiatric symptoms are due to a defect in ourselves.
4. People familiar with Indian philosophy may be open to the notion that we do not have complete free will, and this could be leveraged to help with compliance and treatment.
5. Adding culturally acceptable strategies, such as meditation and yoga, might help patients establish better rapport with the physician and better compliance.

Beena: Abusive Relationships, Depression, and Conversion Disorder

Case History

Beena, a married 23-year-old South Asian-born United States (U.S.) citizen, was medically hospitalized at an Epilepsy Monitoring Unit (EMU) to determine presence of a seizure disorder. After video and electroencephalography, (EEG) recording during her episodes showed no epileptiform discharges, her neurologist diagnosed her as having psuedoseizures and requested psychiatric consultation. The psychiatric consultant examined the patient and spoke to her parents at bedside with her permission.

Beena was born in a South Asian country. When she was 6 years old, her parents moved with her brother and her to the U.S. Beena was married at the age of 16 to an undocumented immigrant from her native country, who was also living in the U.S. This was a marriage arranged by her family. This man was the son of her father's former employer in their native country. Beena was living with her husband in her parents' home. Her husband applied for an immigrant visa through his marriage to her. However, he was arrested for past illegal status in the U.S. and was deported to his native country. Beena had her first seizure at the age of 17, three days after her husband was deported. The seizure occurred following a telephone conversation with her husband's family, who wanted her to return to her native country and live with her husband. The seizure lasted approximately 30 minutes. No medical evaluation was done as the family labeled it as stress.

Subsequently, Beena went to her native country to live with her husband, who was staying at his father's home. Her father-in-law took away her passport and enforced strict house rules and punishment if not followed. Her husband and her in-laws abused her both physically and verbally for not behaving, communicating in a culturally inappropriate way, or for not maintaining family values and tradition. Beena found herself trapped in her in-laws' house. She was not allowed to go outside alone and was not allowed to talk to her family members. Beena was reportedly treated like a servant. At various times, she had hot water thrown on her or was locked out of the house on cold nights. Beena stayed with her husband for 5 years. During this time, she had multiple episodes of seizures. Based on the clinical history, she was diagnosed with a seizure disorder in her native country and was started on antiepileptic medications. Finally, after 5 years of stay in her in-laws' house, Beena's older brother rescued her and brought her back to the U.S. Beena lived with her parents and continued to experience seizures, most often following telephone conversations with her husband and / or in-laws. A typical episode would last about 30-60 minutes and was characterized by twitching of eyes, shaking of body and limbs, profuse sweating, and inability to see or hear anything. No loss of consciousness, bowel or bladder incontinence, or tongue biting was noted. As these episodes continued to happen despite being treated with antiepileptics, her primary care physician referred her to the Epilepsy monitoring unit (EMU) for further evaluation.

In the EMU, video-EEG monitoring showed episodes unaccompanied by ictal EEG changes. The episodes were characterized by bilateral flailing of arms and legs and rapid, heavy breathing. A diagnosis of psuedoseizures was made, and her antiepileptic medication (phenytoin) was discontinued. A psychiatric consultation was obtained. The psychiatric consultant made a diagnosis of Conversion Disorder. He arranged for outpatient psychotherapy with a female psychiatrist from the same country and religion as Beena's parents.

Beena agreed to psychiatric treatment and remained adherent. In addition to the above episodes, at the initial evaluation, Beena also endorsed a number of depressive symptoms consistent with the diagnosis of Major Depressive Disorder. She was treated with an antidepressant and received weekly psychotherapy, which included expressive and supportive therapies. Beena was encouraged to talk about her conflicts, mostly issues related to her husband. In the first few sessions, Beena focused on ways to bring her husband back to the U.S. She requested a letter from the therapist to submit to the U.S. Embassy supporting her wish to reunite with him. Gradually, she opened up and discussed her fights and arguments with her husband and later the abuse. However, because of her family values, she was concerned about divorce. Divorce would be unacceptable to her parents and society. As the therapy progressed, she was able to articulate her anger at her situation and her parents' values. Thereafter, she discussed her desire to get out of the relationship, but was also concerned about the shame it would bring to her family, friends, and society. She talked about her difficult sexual relationship with her husband, who was 10 years older than her and the lack of sexual and emotional intimacy. She had never shared this before with anyone as discussion of sex life was taboo. She talked about her mixed feelings toward her father, who made her get married at a young age. She did not want anyone to know about her angry, hateful feelings towards her father-in-law, as this would bring a lot of tension in the family.

Despite treatment adherence, her depressive symptoms worsened. She was psychiatrically hospitalized after she overdosed on her antidepressant medication. The hospitalization helped. She was discharged after a week on a different antidepressant. She continued regular psychotherapy. The therapy focused on Beena's feelings and wishes, rather than the wishes of her family. After months of therapy, Beena reached a decision to file for divorce, which she did unbeknownst to her family. After she had filed for divorce, her depressive symptoms improved dramatically, and the seizure episodes stopped. Eventually, her family learned about the divorce, and this led to arguments and even physical abuse by her own family. However, even with this tremendous amount of stress, she remained seizure free. She improved in other ways as well. Instead of relying on her parents for financial support, she started to work full-time and began preparing to go back to college. She also became more assertive and changed from wearing traditional clothes to Western attire. She stopped psychiatric treatment six months later as she was emotionally stable. Her therapist contacted her a few months later and learned that she was continuing to do well and moving forward as a single woman to achieve her goals in life.

Diagnostic Formulation

The psychological context of Beena's seizures is apparent from the initial precipitating event and subsequent provoking events. The initial seizure episode followed her speaking to her husband and his family soon after his deportation. Many subsequent episodes were following telephone conversations with her husband or in-laws. Based on the clinical history and lack of ictal activity on EEG, a diagnosis of Conversion Disorder was made. A conversion disorder is an expression of an underlying psychological conflict through a somatic symptom, without the patient being consciously aware of it. The fact that the diagnosis of Conversion Disorder had not been made for several years in this patient. That she was incorrectly being treated with antiepileptic medications for a long time is a sad commentary that unconscious stigma against mental illness might have played a role in both the family and the physicians not recognizing it. Many South Asians do not acknowledge emotional distress associated with intra-family conflict and instead channel it through physical symptoms. This is often done without conscious awareness and influenced by the family or society not tolerating emotional symptoms or coping with conflict. From a psychodynamic point of view, it can be formulated that the intrapsychic conflicts regarding her anger at her husband, father-in-law, and parents with regard to her untenable arranged marriage, desire to escape this marriage, and the internalized cultural prohibition against it, found unconscious somatic expression through psuedoseizures. Beena felt trapped in her unsustainable abusive marriage, cultural and family pressures contributed to a sense of powerlessness, and the psuedoseizures were an unconscious somatic expression of her agony. In addition, this behavior provided comfort, attention from family, and personal space as she was allowed to stay in her room and not be bothered by nagging family members.

Management

After the initial psychiatric consultation, Beena was referred to a female therapist with a similar cultural and religious background. This referral was acceptable to Beena and probably played a significant role in establishing a therapeutic relationship. The concept of cultural matching of therapist and patient is helpful for some patients.

In this case, therapy goals were to: provide Beena an opportunity to discuss her feelings with a professional; provide a safe atmosphere that facilitated free emotional expression; provide her a corrective emotional experience that her feelings were reasonable and acceptable by another person; explore, validate, and clarify her conflictual feelings in a safe atmosphere; and empower her to make the needed changes in her life based on her wishes and priorities. This kind of recognition, acknowledgment, and expression of her feelings led to Beena gaining more autonomy in her actions, which ultimately led to diminished need to somatize her negative feelings.

A recurring theme in some South Asian immigrant families is that the elders / first generation immigrants are still clinging to the restrictive cultural norms from their native societies. These individuals may not be willing to give their children the freedom to exercise their choices congruent with the Western society in which they are living. The young adult has to arrive at a different equilibrium with the system (family) by exercising more autonomy. Sometimes, this may lead to emotional distancing or even relationship break up with some people who are not willing to change or be flexible. The major role of the clinician is to provide a safe holding environment in the therapeutic relationship as the patient goes through the distress associated with making these decisions and changes in life.

Summary

Beena is a married 23-year-old female of South Asian descent who was referred for psychiatric management after psuedoseizures were diagnosed following an EMU stay. The patient was subsequently diagnosed with Conversion Disorder and Major Depressive Disorder. A major feature of this case was the emotional distress associated with an unhappy and abusive marriage, and many of Beena's symptoms abated following divorce from her husband.

Teaching Points

1. Psychological conflicts and conflicts with one's family and society may be expressed through physical symptoms. If the clinician recognizes this, it can lead to effective treatment strategies.
2. Helping a patient identify and express suppressed feelings in psychotherapy can lead to a more mature processing of conflictual emotional material and a more adaptive course of action.
3. Different members of immigrant South Asian families may be in different degrees of acculturation in the U.S., and this can lead to system imbalance and family conflicts. Some immigrant parents hold on rigidly to restrictive attitudes of their native societies, and this can be an important source of conflicts to children raised in the U.S.

Sujatha: A Case of Adjustment Disorder Teaches a Psychiatry Resident about South Asian Culture

Case History

Sujatha, a 24-year-old single female of Indian origin, was referred to an outpatient resident-staffed psychiatric clinic for treatment of symptoms of depression and anxiety. The patient was assigned to a Caucasian male, third year psychiatry resident, who requested a female Indian psychiatrist as a supervisor on the case.

Sujatha immigrated from a southern state of India to the United States (U.S.) on a student visa to further her studies in computer technology. She had received a full scholarship from a prestigious institution in a metropolitan city. She was the only Indian female in her class of several male students from the U.S., China, and India. There were two Caucasian females as well. This was the first time she had traveled abroad.

Soon after arrival to the U.S., Sujatha felt like a fish out of water. Everything seemed new and foreign (i.e., language, food, clothes, and people's attitudes). She felt that people were giving her strange looks, as she looked different. She tended to keep to herself, remained quiet in class, and had no friends. She declined the invitation by two Indian male classmates to go to lunch together, but accepted their invitation a few weeks later to go to an Indian temple in the city. She missed her family a lot. She lived in a rental room near the campus and usually ate in the cafeteria by herself. Being a strict vegetarian, she only had a few choices. She found the food bland and started losing weight. Her sleep became restless with frequent awakenings. She was tired during the day and unable to concentrate. She struggled to keep up with schoolwork, but found it shameful to obtain help from friends and teachers. Her academic advisor suggested she receive psychiatric help when her grades began to decline.

There was no personal or family history of mood disorder or any other psychiatric illness. Sujatha was not on any medications and did not have any medical conditions. She reported no history of substance abuse.

Sujatha was the only child of a couple who were professors at a small city university in India. She described them as loving but strict. They expected her to follow the Hindu rituals and family norms. She was expected to be home before sunset, not eat meat or consume alcohol, not smoke or use any drugs, and attend a local temple weekly. She was not allowed to socialize with men. She had never dated. Both parents stressed the importance of preparing oneself for life by receiving a good education and excelling academically. Sujatha always followed home rules and excelled academically.

During the first session with the psychiatry resident, she came in clad in a beige printed sari (a garment worn by females in India that is typically wrapped around the body) with the palloo (the loose end of a sari) draped around her shoulders. Her hair was in a long braid, and she wore no makeup except kohl (eyeliner). She spoke softly and hesitantly, in a heavy Indian accent, and seldom looked directly at the resident. Although her spoken English was correct, it appeared stilted. With tears in her eyes, she told him that she did not want to see a psychiatrist but came in for evaluation and treatment because she feared that it would anger her advisor if she did not. She also hoped that her grades would improve. When the resident asked her why she did not want to come, she said that she was not crazy and was worried what others might think if they found out that she was seeing a psychiatrist. She described her extreme distress with her poor grades. She felt that her parents would be ashamed to know that her academic performance was not up to par. She felt that she had let them down. She admitted to feeling sad and not sleeping well. She missed her home, family, and friends in India. She had no hallucinations or delusions. She denied feeling suicidal.

Sujatha attended psychotherapy sessions regularly and was always on time. While initially she remained shy, sitting at the edge of the chair and barely making eye contact, she started opening up as the therapy progressed. She often asked for advice, which the resident initially was hesitant to give, but then started making some suggestions. To help her slowly adapt to the Western ways, he suggested that she try to make friends with the two Caucasian female classmates and watch news, movies, and other programs on the TV. In the next session, she reported that she followed his advice and had approached these girls and had started eating lunch regularly with them. She brightened up as she related that these classmates had offered to take her shopping for Western clothes. She told him that she was watching news daily, which not only helped her get in touch with what was going on in the world, but also helped her with American pronunciations.

She came to her next session dressed in black pants, a pink top, and a printed long scarf. She entered the resident's office shyly, but smiling. She appeared happy in this session and talked more than she did usually. She asked him if she should go to the temple again with her two male Indian classmates. When questioned about this, she expressed her concern that asking them out might be misunderstood as being too forward and breaking the gender norm. At the resident's suggestion, she invited her female classmates to go along as well. She enjoyed going out with her male and female classmates to the temple and a local restaurant. She learned the meaning of 'going Dutch' for the first time and felt very comfortable with the concept of each person paying for his or her lunch. As time went by, she felt less lonely and became more engaged in school, work, and outside activities. Her sleep, appetite, and concentration also improved. Her grades improved and her teacher pointed out that her assignments were of good quality.

A few sessions later, the resident was surprised to see her wearing bright red lipstick as he had never seen her wear makeup. She volunteered that her friends had helped her choose some cosmetics. He noticed that she wore a red skirt and would smile coyly at times in the following session. She started asking him personal questions about his living situation and personal life. When the resident asked what the source of her questions was, she said she wanted to know him better. The resident handled this situation by stating that he was her doctor and that this was the only information that mattered. Sujatha was very disappointed by this response.

She did not come for the next session. When she returned two weeks later, she was dressed again in pants, top, and scarf. She had brought a small bag with her from which she took out a small steel plate, a few stemless flowers, a red and white strand of twisted threads, a small container of yellowish powder, and some Indian sweets. As he looked quizzically, she explained that an Indian festival called Raksha Bandhan was coming up soon. She explained that Raksha Bandhan is a celebration to honor the bond between a brother and sister and to maintain this bond, the sister ties a sacred thread (also known as Rakhi) around the wrist of the brother. Sujatha requested the resident's permission to tie the thread around his wrist. The resident asked more about the significance of this festival. She explained that the sister prays for her brother's long life and in return, the brother promises to always protect the sister from evil and misfortune. When the resident said that he was not her brother, she shook her head and said that in a way he was because he helped her get adjusted to the life in the U.S. and protected her from sufferings for which she was grateful. At this point, the resident let her tie the thread on his wrist after she put the yellowish powder on his forehead and showered a few flower petals on his head – a sacred ritual in India to offer blessings / gratitude. Following this ritual, she appeared happy and content. She came for one more session during which they decided to end the therapeutic sessions with the understanding that she would contact him if she needed any further psychiatric help.

A few months later, she telephoned the resident to wish him Happy Diwali (Indian / Hindu celebration of lights festival) and related that she was doing much better in her classes.

Diagnostic Formulation

A diagnosis of Adjustment Disorder with depressive symptoms was made and the resident decided to treat her with weekly supportive psychotherapy. The resident explained to her that she was not crazy, but was experiencing challenges with acculturation and difficulty coping with a new place and a demanding school curriculum.

Sujatha's feelings of inadequacy and shame surfaced as her grades dropped. She believed she had let her family down. This is not uncommon in the Eastern culture as education is highly valued, and poor academic performance is considered a failure and an embarrassment to the individual and family. In Eastern cultures, the individual does not exist as an independent and solitary person, but as a member of a collective and cohesive group (i.e., the family). The family is not limited to husband, wife, and their children, but includes extended family members (e.g., grandparents, uncles, aunts, cousins). In this group, various members are interdependent on each other. An achievement of a particular person becomes an achievement and a matter of pride for the entire family. A failure of one individual is perceived as failure of the entire clan with inherent shame attached to it.

Management

To request a supervisor who was familiar with the culture of the patient was appropriate, as the patient the resident was treating was a young woman having trouble adjusting to new surroundings and Western culture. The program director appropriately responded to the resident's request and provided an attending of Indian origin as his supervisor for this case. The resident met with the supervisor weekly for 30 minutes to discuss the case and obtain guidance and training. During these sessions, the attending encouraged him to view problems and solutions related to the case from an Eastern perspective, provided reading material on pertinent topics related to the case, and discussed and answered questions as they came up. The attending never met the patient.

The choice of supportive psychotherapy with first establishing rapport and providing reassurance by explaining that Sujatha was not "crazy," greatly helped to relieve her anxiety and tension. Later, the supportive therapy focused on helping her acculturate by making appropriate suggestions, which helped her with her loneliness and to learn the nuances of the American culture. It helped her build a supportive network around her with the help of the two Indian males and two Caucasian female colleagues. As her grades improved, so did the feelings of inadequacy and shame. The resident decided to make some suggestions and gave advice because most Indian patients expect that from their physicians. These individuals respect their physicians and implicitly follow their advice.

The shyness and coyness that Sujatha displayed earlier in her therapy sessions is often seen in young South Asian women, who have been raised with strict traditional values and not exposed to the Western world. Girls are usually not allowed to talk to boys outside the close family or strangers as it is considered uncultured. Similarly, making minimal eye contact during conversations with boys or strangers, draping the end of the sari around the shoulder, and wearing minimal make up, are also valued as being respectful, polite, and highly traditional. As seen in this case, the shyness usually fades away with time.

The transformation in Sujatha's attire and her desire to get to know the resident at a personal level was probably a sexual transference. Sujatha probably felt embarrassed about this leading to her absence from the next session. In many parts of India, girls are not allowed to talk or socialize with men. Being in the presence of a male therapist with whom she was sharing personal issues and receiving helpful suggestions may have triggered romantic feelings. It is probable that she took a break to process and sort out her feelings and finally chose a strategy, which to her was healthy and most accepting. The tying of the sacred thread on the resident's wrist helped her bind her anxiety related to the emerging sexual feelings toward the resident and reestablish a different bond, that of a protector.

In some, acculturation and adaptation is less of an issue these days, especially for those who have been raised in large metropolitan cities in India. However, this remains a problem for those coming from smaller cities and towns and for those who have never traveled abroad. Therapists need to be cognizant of these facts and treat their cases empathically.

Summary

Sujatha is a 24-year-old single female of Indian descent who was treated for Adjustment Disorder with outpatient psychotherapy. Sujatha came to the US for higher education and struggled to adapt to the new culture. Her strict upbringing in India created a conflict with her cultural norms and changes / demands of the Western culture. She was referred for psychiatric evaluation and treatment when her grades declined and she began experiencing depressive symptoms. Supportive psychotherapy helped her overcome many of these handicaps resulting in better grades and improved mood. With the support and guidance of a psychiatry resident, who was being supervised by an attending physician with expertise in the South Asian culture, the patient showed an overall psychological growth.

Teaching Points

1. Training in cultural psychiatry should be part of residency training.
2. Residents should request supervision and guidance from experts when working with a patient from a different culture.
3. While most South Asians prefer pharmacotherapy and a biological approach for evaluation and management, not all require medications. A thorough assessment into the root cause of the psychiatric or psychological issue is essential to decide on the best line of treatment.

Prakash: Successful Acculturation through Legal Intervention

Case History

Prakash, a 35-year-old recently married male of South Asian descent, was court-mandated to complete a psychiatric evaluation due to a charge of sexual abuse of a minor. Prakash had a Master's degree in Information Technology and had moved to the United States (U.S.) in search of better job opportunities.

Prakash felt confident that he would quickly find a job in the U.S. as his older brother with similar qualification had moved to the U.S. more than a decade ago and was doing very well. The plan was for Prakash and his wife to live with his brother and his family until Prakash found a job and was financially sufficient. The brother's family included his wife and their 11-year-old daughter, Nisha. Prakash's brother was happy to help and felt responsible being the older sibling. His wife agreed, but preferred it be a short stay, as she wanted her space and did not want to foster dependence. Ultimately, they all lived together in a three-bedroom apartment. Prakash and his wife continued to stay with his brother even after he had a job. Prakash was healthy with no known medical or psychiatric history. He did not drink, smoke, or use illicit drugs. There was no family history of psychiatric illness.

Nisha, Prakash's niece, was an excellent student and attended a private school close to their home in New York. During a sexual awareness education class that Nisha was attending, the teacher asked if anyone had been inappropriately touched in a way that made them feel uncomfortable.

A few raised their hands and Nisha was one of them. When asked to describe, Nisha reported the following:

"I was watching an Indian movie with my parents, my uncle Prakash, and my aunt. During this time, I was sitting on my uncle's lap. He tapped on my thighs several times during the movie when funny scenes were on. I was uncomfortable, but I did not say anything. This was the only time I had experienced this kind of uncomfortable feeling."

The teacher reported this situation to the guidance counselor, who involved the social services of New York and later the police. One afternoon, the police showed up at Prakash's workplace, handcuffed him, and took him to the precinct. On hearing this, Nisha's father immediately contacted an Indian attorney to determine what was going on and to represent his brother. Prakash presented to the judge the next morning with charges of sexual abuse of a minor. The Indian attorney explained to the judge the Indian cultural norm of extended family members living together. He also explained that it is not uncommon for adults to hold children on the lap or sit close to them while watching movies or reading stories. These type of behaviors are often considered expressions of warmth, affection, and / or family togetherness. However, the judge ordered Nisha, her parents, and Prakash to be evaluated by a psychiatrist and a letter be sent to him every month for twelve months with details about the findings. In addition, Prakash was not allowed to have any contact with Nisha until the judge lifted this restriction. Prakash was only released when an Indian psychiatrist was identified, who was willing to evaluate him regularly and send a letter to the judge every month. Prakash and his wife were also court ordered to find their own apartment and not visit Nisha's family.

The psychiatrist met with the family and developed a plan to meet monthly with Prakash and his wife. There would also be sessions with Nisha and Nisha's parents, as a group and individually. The psychiatrist took consent from all individuals regarding sending a letter to the judge every month. Even though Prakash was the primary person to be evaluated and educated, the case involved working with the entire family. The psychiatrist noted that this was an unusual situation, which she had not dealt with in her practice, but was willing to carry out the Judge's mandate if the family was willing to cooperate. The psychiatrist emphasized that Prakash and his wife not visit Nisha at school or home. The school was also informed that Nisha was not be picked up by her uncle at any time.

The psychiatrist met with Nisha to explore the event. She underwent a comprehensive evaluation and was ruled out for major mental illness and intellectual disabilities. Nisha was confused as to what she had done wrong that got her uncle in trouble. The psychiatrist concluded that Nisha had always received a lot of attention from her parents and extended family members and was innocently looking for attention from her classmates and her teacher.

The psychiatrist met with Nisha's parents who felt angry and guilty that they had not educated Nisha about living together with extended family members, as it was culturally acceptable in Indian families. Nisha's mother was relieved that the judge mandated Prakash not to have any contact with Nisha and blamed him for the trouble in her family.

On evaluation of Prakash, the psychiatrist noted that he was a smart young man who found it appropriate to stay with his older brother and his family for an extended time as they would have done in India. He had made no effort to get independent housing since moving to the U.S., although his wife was encouraging him to do so. He blamed the American education system, legal system, and culture for this current legal trouble.

Prakash's wife, who never wanted to stay with her husband's brother and family, blamed her husband and his brother for the ongoing state of affairs. However, she was concerned that her husband's encounter with the legal system would blemish his career. She was also concerned about response from other family members and friends should this news leak out. Nevertheless, she trusted her husband and completely believed he was innocent.

In summary, a once cohesive family was now in chaos.

After the evaluations, the psychiatrist sent her first letter to the judge stating that Prakash did not have any evidence of mental illness or character pathology. There was no history of alcohol, illicit drug abuse, or gambling. Nisha was safe and well protected by the parents. There was no evidence of sexual abuse. The judge accepted the letter.

Every month the psychiatrist met with individual family members and discussed the issues that had hurt the family and strategies to improve relationships. The psychiatrist noted that Prakash, although defiant initially, was willing to be educated about socially / sexually appropriate behaviors. Nisha's mother took the longest to heal from the event, as she was very upset about any trauma the event might have caused Nisha. On the other hand, Nisha was quick to learn about unacceptable sexual advances, which she repeatedly said her uncle had not meant to do. Over twelve months, each individual member of the family followed Nisha in accepting this event as a learning experience. At the end of the year, the judge lifted the restrains on Prakash. The whole family thanked the judge for understanding their culture and giving them an opportunity to learn about American culture, its norms, and its laws.

Diagnostic Formulation

All family members underwent comprehensive psychiatric evaluations and major mental illness was ruled out in all of them. In addition, Nisha was also evaluated for intellectual difficulties given concern that an adult may have taken advantage of an intellectually disabled child.

She was not found to have any kind of intellectual difficulties or learning disorder. The appropriate diagnosis for all adults in this case is acculturation difficulty. Nisha's father, being the oldest in the family, felt responsible to have his younger brother and his wife stay with them. Nisha's mother, being more practical, felt their family responsibility should not be carried too long. Prakash, being a younger brother, felt entitled to continue family life in the U.S. just the way he would have in India. Prakash's wife, on the other hand, was eager to have her own place and live independently. No psychiatric diagnosis was given for Nisha as the psychiatrist felt she had innocently embellished a culturally appropriate incident.

Management

Psychiatrists may come across cases where the identified patient may not have a diagnosis; however, the goal may be to address the family issues that brought the patients(s) into psychiatric care. In this case, the psychiatrist had to explore the alleged sexual abuse that Nisha claimed.

Nisha was evaluated for any kind of intellectual disabilities, which may have led her to become a victim of sexual advances. The psychiatrist explored if Nisha's parents were negligent in any way. Prakash was carefully evaluated for any such accusations, present or in the past. Nisha's mother was helpful in giving the psychiatrist details about the extended family history in India, as well as in the U.S. It was comforting for the psychiatrist that this was a loving family, which had become a victim of innocent and culturally accepted sequence of events.

The therapeutic relationship with Nisha, her parents, Prakash, and Prakash's wife, greatly improved when the psychiatrist non-judgmentally, without labeling or blaming, educated everyone individually and as a group about the American culture, laws, and legal system. She also spoke of the importance of educating children about sexuality. In addition, she educated each family member on roles and responsibilities of protecting children, who are often vulnerable. This led to the family trusting the psychiatrist and feeling safe in a new culture.

A culturally sensitive attorney and judge were extremely helpful to the family. Although the mandate given by the judge had to be carried out, the psychiatrist used creative and culturally syntonic ideas to keep the family integrity once it was identified that the vulnerable child, Nisha, was safe.

Acceptance of emotional issues does not come very easily to Indian patients. In addition, reluctance is also secondary to stigma, shame, and embarrassment. They feel ashamed and embarrassed to seek treatment for a problem they "should have easily overcome within the family." In addition, the treatment was mandated by a powerful legal system, which was frightening to the family. In addition to the individual evaluation of Prakash, family therapy focused on Nisha was essential. This treatment was comprehensive and included non-traditional psychotherapy, which included education and readings about American cultural norms.

Prakash expected the psychiatrist to give him concrete directions. This is not uncommon among Asian-Indians. They expect the psychiatrist to be proactive and provide concrete advice. Authority figures are held in high regard and greatly respected. Prakash, although initially defiant, eventually learned to voice his feelings of guilt for having caused unintentionally turmoil in his brother's family life. The psychiatrist also helped the family reunite by giving the adults permission to have phone contact with each other. The psychiatrist took an authoritarian role and provided guidance to maintain the family integrity. She also helped Prakash maintain his job. At Prakash's request and permission, she contacted his supervisor and explained to him the sequence of events and the cultural nuances associated with this incident. Involvement of family in psychiatric treatment can be tricky as some overdo and others are reluctant to involve family members. Clinicians should understand individual family dynamics and try to strike the balance between keeping the treatment on the individual and engaging family members appropriately. This should be discussed and negotiated with the identified patient at the start of treatment.

Summary

Prakash is a 35-year-old married male of South Asian descent who was legally- and psychiatrically-cleared following court-mandated psychiatric evaluation on a charge of sexual abuse of a minor. He saw the psychiatrist for over a year, and it was determined that the inciting incident involved behavior deemed inappropriate by Western culture, but not sexual abuse. Reluctant at first to engage for fear of being diagnosed with a mental illness, Prakash eventually accepted treatment focused on education and guidance. The treatment plan involved Prakash and all involved family members. There was no labeling or blaming, but the psychiatrist skillfully worked on uniting the family and educating them on issues that got them into trouble.

Teaching Points

1. Acculturation difficulties are present in many different forms. It is not always about adjusting to new food, language, and religious practices. In this case, acculturation difficulties involved being unaware of certain customs and practices and engaging in behaviors that were deemed inappropriate in the country of settlement.

2. As clinicians, it is important to be attentive and sensitive to cultural explanations and when in doubt to consult people / experts of the same culture.
3. Education on acculturation is a process. The psychiatrist spent time working with all family members individually and as a group, listening to them and educating them. Sometimes, the clinician may have to focus on the entire family.

Zoha: Group and Individual Psychotherapy following a Life of Trauma

Case History

Zoha is a 38-year-old 1.5-generation South Asian-American single female who first pursued psychiatric treatment in her late twenties wanting to address the following concerns: communication issues with her parents, conflict with employers, cultural conflict with dating, and pressure to get married. The term 1.5 generation is used to describe a person born outside the United States (U.S.) who immigrated with their parents to the U.S. at a young age.

Zoha received services through a pro bono counseling project focused on delivering wellness care to South Asians and was a member of a women's wellness group. The counseling project was developed to offer a space for South Asian-Americans to identify stressors, learn new coping strategies, and develop a support network with women who have faced similar cultural issues. Zoha had to overcome her own biases about joining a group comprised of women who identify as South Asian-American. She was concerned about being judged, gaining acceptance, and trusting the confidentiality from the other women in the group. However, she soon realized that the issues she wanted to address during the seven-week women's group were similar to others in the group. Many of the conversations focused on culture clash and gender-based societal pressures. After the women's group ended, Zoha entered into individual therapy with one of the group facilitators, a clinical social worker. Over the course of 10 years, Zoha and her therapist discussed numerous past traumas. Symptoms of Post-Traumatic Stress Disorder (PTSD) and depression were prominent, and a great deal of internalized anger and conflict emerged. This case study focuses on sexual trauma, generational violence, and familial conflict.

Zoha was born in South Asia. She was brought to the U.S. by her adoptive parents, who are also her maternal aunt and uncle. It was believed that her adoptive parents were infertile, and thus Zoha's biological parents, her adoptive mother's sister and brother-in-law, agreed to give their second child to her adoptive parents. This practice of bearing a child to give to an infertile family member is inline with familial adoption norms in some South Asian countries. Within a few years of bringing infant Zoha to the U.S., her adoptive parents were able to conceive and carry two biological sons to term. The ability of Zoha's adoptive parents to bear two sons after adopting Zoha caused distrust and anger with the biological parents and the larger extended family still in South Asia.

During individual therapy, Zoha described witnessing severe violence in her adoptive family. Her adoptive father was physically, financially, and emotionally abusive to her adoptive mother. Zoha and her younger brothers were witness to the abuse but not physically abused themselves. She also described her father as playful and generous with her and her brothers when they were children. He would always buy them gifts, sent them to expensive private schools, and took them on trips around the world. Zoha's adoptive family in the U.S. lived an upper-class existence and maintained an image of wealth and luxury. This kind of "success" was reportedly important to the family.

Zoha's adoptive mother described her youth as being raised in poverty with several siblings. The siblings, who are all still close, have become financially successful; the brothers by attaining an education and career, the sisters by marrying into wealthy families. The adoptive mother reported being physically abused as a child. Zoha's adoptive father, the youngest of several children, bragged of being the smartest and wealthiest of his siblings. He shared stories of beating animals and servants who would not listen to him as a youth. After his father passed away, Zoha's adoptive father became the patriarch of the family, even though he was the youngest of the siblings. The grandfather had accrued wealth and built a large home with multiple wings in which all of his children and their families could live. Some of the adult children remained in South Asia, while others moved out of the country.

During her elementary years, Zoha would seek attention from her peers and teachers. She would often cry to her teachers when other girls did not want play with her. She told some of her teachers about the violence in her home. However, she had no recollection of an intervention from protective services or the police. Zoha described one younger brother as having several physical ailments as a child. Her father viewed his son's illness as a weakness and would berate and mock him for his physical symptoms. The youngest brother would often retreat when his parents were fighting and would avoid getting involved.

At the same time, Zoha's biological parents in South Asia were becoming increasingly concerned that Zoha was becoming too "Americanized." While they were aware of the domestic violence in the home, the biological parents were more concerned about Zoha Western dress, interest in boys, and that things could worsen as she approached puberty. They did not believe Zoha would be a "good South Asian" if she remained in the U.S.

During a yearly visit back to her native hometown, the biological family decided they wanted to take custody of Zoha to teach her how to be a "proper" South Asian girl. She was 12 years old at the time. When the adoptive family refused, the biological family kidnapped Zoha and took her to the tribal-controlled area of South Asia where all of the extended family lived.

Over the next five years, Zoha was held against her will in her biological parents' home with her older and younger brothers. She wanted to go back to her parents in the U. S., but the biological family refused to let her leave. The adoptive family tried to convince the biological family to send her back, but did not take legal action to bring her back. They ended up leaving South Asia without her and tried to convince the family to let her come back.

During the time in her country of birth, Zoha endured beatings from both of her biological parents for not following traditions or for reading novels by American writers. Zoha was also sexually molested by her older biological brother during this time. When she finally spoke out about the incestuous molestation, her biological parents intervened and punished the brother. As time went on, the parents believed their son had repented because he became more devout in his religious practices. The biological parents then turned their rage to Zoha and blamed her for the molestation.

They also falsely accused Zoha of being promiscuous and enticing boys with her "American" ways.

The molestation stopped, but the beatings and accusations continued for several years. During this entire time, Zoha's adoptive parents had been trying to convince her biological parents to return Zoha back to them. The night before she was allowed to return to the U.S., Zoha prayed and asked God "To make her life useful." Finally, at the age of 18, she was put on a plane to return to the U. S. to rejoin her adoptive family.

Once Zoha returned to the U.S. at the age of 18, her adoptive father enrolled her into college and encouraged her to forget about the past and focus on her future. The family was not open to therapy and believed the best way to deal with the previous trauma was to leave it in the past. Zoha used the counseling services at the college at a high frequency and managed to graduate. She then attended graduate school and obtained a Master's degree. Even during this time, she continued to use the counseling services and gradually built a support network of friends.

Currently, Zoha is living on her own and employed in a career in the mental health profession. She has not communicated with her biological parents since returning from her native country. She often discusses her relationships with her adoptive mother in therapy and works on boundaries that will help her be a support for her mother. Zoha's father has severe health issues and her mother continues to live with her husband. The verbal and financial abuse continues, but the physical abuse declined as the adoptive father's health declined. Zoha feels she has come a long way in addressing the traumas and creating a different life for herself. While she understands that it is difficult for her adoptive mother to separate or divorce her abusive husband because of cultural expectations, she continues to encourage her mother to seek professional help. Zoha reports positive relationships with both her adoptive brothers, but notes they are not as close as she wishes they were.

Diagnostic Formulation

Zoha has never been psychiatrically hospitalized, but has been in some form of therapy over the last twenty years. She has been on antidepressants at various points. Zoha exhibited several features of PTSD and depression, such as episodes of persistent sadness, anxiety, anhedonia, lack of motivation, insomnia, feelings of hopelessness, and low self-worth.

While Zoha did not describe or exhibit the more common symptoms of PTSD, such as flashbacks or nightmares, she exhibited or endorsed the following symptoms: reactive angry reactions, rumination of scenarios in which she felt wronged, inability to maintain healthy boundaries, identification with the abuser, blaming of the person being abused, and inability to cognitively process how her behaviors were resulting in unintended consequences. Zoha was able to identify triggers, which prompted feelings of anxiety with a flight or fight response, and then subsequent days of intense emotions.

The responses to triggers would vacillate between depressive and angry responses; the underlying depression was intermittently treated with antidepressants by her physician, but never monitored by a psychiatrist. Zoha was not resistant to seeing a psychiatrist, but the ease of accessing antidepressants through her primary care physician, and her inconsistency with taking the medication, influenced her decision.

Zoha's family further stigmatized her for taking medications to cope with her mental illness, which was another barrier she learned to overcome. While Zoha's adoptive parents are college-educated, they still had many beliefs about mental illness rooted in cultural beliefs. While several passages in the Quran, one of the holy books in Islam, discuss the value of taking care of your mental health, there is a belief within Islam that a spiritual abandonment or lack of faith in Islam will cause depression or an imbalance in one's wellbeing. As such, many Imams, or spiritual leaders, will advise adherence to one's daily prayers or daily reading of the Quran. Islam also has beliefs about the supernatural and spirit beings or jinns, which some Muslims believe exist among humans. The whispers of evil jinns are believed to be the whisperings of Satan who will lead followers away from Islam. Schizophrenia is commonly believed to be a result of a possession, and thus praying over a person to drive the jinn out of the body is still practiced in some Muslim countries.

The depressive symptoms she exhibited started with reports of sadness, excessive eating, and irritability with her family and close friends. At one point, she reported daily crying spells, angry outbursts at work, feelings of hopelessness, and victimization. With the increase in symptoms, it was recommended that she see a psychiatrist or her primary care provider for medication. She eventually went back on antidepressants and was compliant. After her mood stabilized, she was able to make significant changes to address situations exacerbating her depressive symptoms.

Management

Zoha entered a pro bono women's wellness group wanting to connect with other South Asian women who were not from the same country of origin or religious background. She was not sure if she fit in with other South Asian women and was concerned with how she would be perceived. The level of violence in her past, the incestuous sexual abuse, and additional trauma were significant. During the intake for the group, the facilitators almost excluded her from the group, with concerns her trauma may be too severe. An honest discussion with Zoha about the concerns helped the facilitators with giving Zoha more agency over her decision.

The group validated several experiences that were similar within the culture-gender expectations: difficulties communicating with parents, pressures to marry, classism, colorism, and internalized racism. During the group, Zoha disclosed the history of her kidnap and physical and sexual violence. The group was empathetic and validated the strengths they saw in her. The experience of having women of South Asian origin validate her experience, and not criticize or judge her, was impactful for Zoha. While she had told her story to many others, the safety of the group provided a different type of validation and recognition of her strengths that she had not experienced before. In the women's wellness group, Zoha was viewed as a woman of strength, not as a victim. This was a critical shift in how Zoha began to view herself.

At the end of the group, Zoha asked if she could continue with individual therapy with one of the facilitators of the group. Since the group had ended, the therapist agreed to take Zoha on as a client. In the individual sessions, Zoha had a pattern of storytelling, wanting to share every detail of her adoptive parents, history of abuse, friends who mocked her, work colleagues who devalued her, or past physical relationships with men. In all of these situations, she was most comfortable with spending time telling the stories and sharing details of what each person in the story did or said, and centered herself as the victim in the stories. The victim role and chaotic environments had become the norm to Zoha; she gravitated towards people with unstable lives and unhealthy relationships, or people who wanted her to "fix" them. Zoha's storytelling would then include the lives of others, which caused a lack of trust with her friends. Her friends and family also saw her as comical and dramatic, which Zoha found belittling.

During therapy, a combination of cognitive-behavioral strategies, mindfulness, and emotional freedom techniques were used to address the issues both from her past and present. PTSD was addressed with a combination of tapping or emotional freedom techniques, writing, and walking on a treadmill for a few minutes during therapy.

Cognitive-behavioral therapy focused on unpacking the negative thoughts and messages Zoha had formulated from the years of abuse. The dichotomy of "Good Girl" vs. "Bad Girl" was deeply woven in her identity and that of cultural and religious beliefs, which she had also internalized at a deeper subconscious level. Zoha rebelled against some of the traditional South Asian views of a "Good Girl" which she described as: quiet, obedient, quick-witted, slim, married at a young age, a virgin, educated but not career-oriented, a dutiful wife, a mother and daughter, religious, and able to put on an appearance of perfection to anyone outside the home. The "Bad Girl" descriptors included: talkative, opinionated, unmarried, dating and sexually active, career-oriented, nonreligious, and openly discussing problems and issues. While Zoha did not believe in all the "Good Girl" qualifications, she still wanted to be seen as a "Good South Asian" and admired by her family. Individual therapy focused on how to be a "Good Daughter" while maintaining her identity and values and not allowing herself to be abused. Therapy also focused on setting boundaries with friends and family and holding on to relationships, which were mutually nurturing.

Zoha was greatly hurt that her family in South Asia had not only forgiven her abusive brother, but also viewed him with admiration. The gender bias favoring males in South Asian countries and the belief that repentance and adherence to Islamic practices has absolved the perpetrator of his wrongdoings, contributed to the family's forgiveness of Zoha's brother. In addition to her individual and group therapy, Zoha wrote blogs about her experiences and served as a speaker at story-telling events. This creative outlet offered a means to tell her story with an engaged audience, and with complete control in how the narrative was delivered.

Summary

Zoha is a 38-year-old 1.5-generation South Asian-American single female actively engaged in individual and group psychotherapy for treatment of PTSD and depression. This case brings to light the complexities of trauma, family, cultural taboos, cultural expectations, patriarchy, and gender expectations. Zoha has lived experiences that may have devastated others, yet her fierce determination to heal and to help others has guided her path towards health and wellness. The path to healing is ongoing. Through talk therapy, emotionally freedom tapping techniques, and movement therapy, this woman continues to nurture the internal harms, while disrupting harmful patterns in her family.

Teaching Points

1. Discussion of incest and domestic violence are difficult as family members often do not support the person and may disown them. Therapy should be multipronged and address not only the trauma, healing, and emotional issues, but empowerment and validation of skills and self-worth, so that the patient can create a strong support system. In this case, while Zoha felt rejected by people in her immediate community, she felt accepted by her support group peers and by the larger community. The South-Asian women's group, and having a therapist of South Asian origin, offered her a healing space for validation and support to build on her strengths and move towards her goals.
2. Familial adoptions are traditional and a way of supporting infertile family members. Usually, no paperwork is filed in these adoptions, and it is often a family secret. With the advances of

fertility treatments, this type of familial adoption is becoming less common

3. South Asian culture tends to hold women to certain ideals such as having a slim figure, a light skin tone, being educated but not working for an income, being married, and having children. However, with increasing globalization, many women are caught between traditional values and modernity, struggling to attain a balance. It is important for clinicians to be more inter-culturally and globally aware.

Leela: The Impact of an Abusive Marriage on an Otherwise Healthy Woman

Case History

Leela, a 49-year-old widowed, remarried female of South Asian descent who sought counselling in the setting of a difficult second marriage. Her goals were to learn ways to regulate her emotions and improve her self-confidence and self-esteem.

Leela came from an upper middle class family. She and her siblings were raised in a loving environment. She did very well in school and college and participated in a number of extracurricular activities. After obtaining Master's degree, she worked as an executive in a multinational company. Her family and friends described her as "dynamic, vivacious, and energetic." She was very well liked and respected by her friends and peers.

Leela is a practicing Hindu and based her principles on religious values. She has had two marriages. Her first marriage was short and lasted for only a couple of years. Her husband, who worked abroad, died suddenly of a heart attack. At the time of his death, Leela was 8 months pregnant. A year after his death, she re-married her deceased husband's younger brother and they had three children. There were strong personality differences between her first and second husband. While both were born and raised in rural India and came from a lower middle class family, her first husband was independent and prioritized his relationship with his wife. Her second husband was domineering and suspicious towards her and had an enmeshed relationship with his parents. He often leaned on his parents for every-day decision making. This led to Leela's in-laws constantly interfering in their marriage, which in turn led to frequent fights and even physical abuse.

After many years of a difficult marriage, Leela sought counselling. In her first session, Leela noted that she had endured violence for most of her second marriage (at that time 18 years in length). She stated that she tolerated the abuse and justified it stating that it was his possessiveness and immense love for her that made him behave this way. However, over the years, by observing and discussing with friends and other family members, Leela realized that her marriage was unhealthy. This led her to initiate therapy for the first time. Her husband accompanied her to a few sessions. He was supportive of her seeking counselling because he had always believed that she was the one with problems. He stopped accompanying her after a few sessions, as he believed the therapist favoured Leela.

During therapy sessions, Leela shared very fond memories of her life with her deceased husband. After his death, she was devastated and felt hopeless. She had no desire to live or move forward in life. She attempted to end her life on a few occasions, but was never successful. During this time, her present husband stood by her and supported her not just as a brother-in-law but also as a good friend. Against the wishes of his extended family members, but with the support of his parents, he decided to marry Leela. Leela also agreed to this marriage, as she felt helpless as a widow raising a child single-handedly. At first, she felt indebted and grateful to him, but later as she suffered the physical and emotional abuse, she regretted her decision. Her relationship with her in-laws was also very difficult, as they were extremely demanding and controlling. They too mistreated her (physical, verbal, and emotional abuse) and insulted her in front of her family and friends using derogatory remarks. Her husband never supported her and on the contrary mistreated her along with his parents.

Leela noted that the last few years had been the most difficult of her life. Her husband had suffered severe financial loss in his business. She truly believed that he did not have the entrepreneurial skills to build a business from scratch and encouraged him to get other jobs. He refused and attributed his losses to racial discrimination. He had taken several loans and had difficulty repaying. Leela, on the other hand, had a very good position with a multinational company. She was well liked and respected by her peers. She had been promotioned several times due to her exemplary performance and received a substantial increase in her salary. She was financially supporting her family. Her husband was jealous of her role and high quality work performance and expressed this through emotional and physical abuse. Leela's husband drank regularly and would often become violent after consumption of alcohol.

Diagnostic Formulation

Leela was formulated as having Adjustment Disorder with depressed mood. Her symptoms of sadness and hopelessness were related to her stressful and abusive marriage. There was no family history of psychiatric illness or a past personal history of psychiatric illness. Leela's mood changes were contained and related only to the stressful relationship with her husband. Outside this, at work, with other family members, and socially, she was active, productive, and engaged.

Despite her very progressive outlook, Leela was conservative on certain issues like cultural norms, traditions, and status in her community / society. For a long time, she put up with her husband's dominance, made excuses for his abuse, and tolerated the suffering to keep her family intact. Hinduism, like many other religions, is a male dominated religion. She accepted this and saw her primary duty as serving her husband and taking care of her family.

Even though Leela's husband broke the traditional custom by marrying a widow, he struggled to accept his wife as an equal and partner. He considered himself the breadwinner and decision maker. It was unbearable for him to accept the role reversal. He displaced his jealousy, frustration, and anger on his wife through violence and intimidation

Management

Psychotherapy with some South Asian clients can be challenging and complex with the therapist having to break some boundaries from mainstream Western models of psychotherapy. While in both Eastern and Western models of psychotherapy, establishing therapeutic rapport, having a holistic approach, and being non-judgmental and respectful is important, clinicians may have to wear multiple hats while working with some South Asian clients. Clinicians may have to play the roles of a therapist, teacher, mentor, advocate, and authority figure. It is extremely vital to demonstrate a sense of being in the "here and now" and navigate the sessions as the patient opens up. With several Indian languages, it might be equally beneficial if the clinician is fluent in the language the client speaks or, in settings where this is a limitation, use an interpreter who can speak the language. In this case, a therapeutic rapport was quickly established as Leela identified with her therapist as they spoke the same language. The Western education of the Indian therapist also appealed to Leela as she felt she could relate well to the therapist.

Once the therapeutic relationship was established, the therapist developed a comprehensive treatment plan. The plan included:

- Education about victims' rights, safety, and legal intervention when needed.
- Education on violence / abuse and the negative impact it can have on the victim and other family members, including children.
- Patient-centered, solution focused supportive and modified cognitive behavior therapy to treat symptoms of depression, allow expression of anger effectively, decrease feelings of responsibility for the abusive behaviour of the perpetrator, boost self-esteem, decrease isolation, increase social network, and engage in community activities.
- Set up safety plans for the protection of self and children. This included preparing an emergency safety bag with essentials (e.g., passports, clothing, school reports, birth certificates, education certificates, marriage certificates, money, and medications.

The therapist's primary approach was through psychoeducation, occasional positive self-disclosure when appropriate (e.g., personal experiences to motivate or encourage patient), and a proactive, advocacy-oriented therapeutic style. The therapist's authoritative advisory point of orientation was very successful. This should be considered a norm when working with South Asian clients who rely heavily on the therapist for concrete advice and opinion on decision-making. Authoritative figures are highly respected and therefore a directive approach often helps to establish a successful therapeutic alliance. The primary orientation of therapy was person-centered with a solution-focused approach. Modified cognitive behavioural therapy was introduced with structured homework assignments and exercise to follow. In addition to individual counselling, the therapist also worked extensively with Leela's parents and siblings, helping them problem solve and provide support and education.

The therapist creatively operationalized the sessions to effectively create a safe and trusting environment. For instance, rather than just validating thoughts and feelings, the therapist reflected on nonverbal behaviours and conflictual feelings and thoughts. In addition, the therapist used visual imagery, metaphors, proverbs, and analogies that were culture specific, had symbolical connection, and meaning for the client. In one session, the therapist used the foundations and the teachings of Bagavad Gita to help the client break from her distorted thoughts and negativity towards life. The Bhagavad Gita is one the holy books of Hinduism and provides a framework for growth and spirituality. Some of the teachings of Bagavad Gita that were discussed included:

- Whatever has happened is for your good.
- Whatever is happening will go on well and lead towards a closure and contentment.
- Whatever will happen will also be for your betterment.
- Do not repent for what you have lost.

After about 20 sessions, there was a remarkable change in Leela. Her symptoms of anxiety and depression had totally reduced to minimal or almost none. She was promoted to a higher position at work, which provided her lots of benefits that allowed her to make decisions that she hesitated before. She finally decided to move out of the marriage and take full custody of her children.

In the last 10 years, Leela has transformed into a strong willed, independent, successful and ambitious woman. She is confident and comfortable in her new role. She moved out of her country about 16 years ago after her second marriage. In addition, there are no particular challenges or obstacles noted in her acculturation and assimilation process since she moved to a foreign country. She has adapted well and has achieved the socioeconomic status that she hoped when she left her homeland. Her children are doing well and she is successful at work.

Summary

Leela is a 45-year-old widowed, remarried South Asian woman who was diagnosed with Adjustment Disorder with depressed mood in the setting of an abusive marriage. She remained subservient for some time and tolerated the abuse to keep her family intact. However, as the abuse continued, she decided to seek professional help. She learned several coping and confidence boosting strategies in therapy, which greatly helped improve her self-esteem and ability to function and flourish independently. Therapy was multipronged and included safety planning, support, education, and solution focused. The therapist served as not only a counsellor, but also the patient's mentor, teacher, and advocate, which greatly helped in establishing and maintaining therapeutic alliance.

Teaching Points

1. The clinician may have to creatively and effectively move in and out of multiple roles, such as an authority figure, therapist, doctor, mentor, teacher, life coach, and advocate. The ability to assume these roles compassionately, genuinely, and sensitively is the key to effective therapeutic outcomes. This is almost a necessity in most cases that involves South Asian clients.
2. Culturally, South Asians follow or represent a collectivistic society. Extended families can play a very significant support system for the wellbeing of the individual. The involvement of the family members provides an extended support system.
3. Targeted self-disclosure, when appropriate, may be necessary at times. The role of the therapist when working with South Asian clients is viewed as an authority / mentor. The patient looks to the provider for direction and guidance. Use this constructively by

self-disclosing certain life events that could have been challenging and your coping strategies. This disclosure will strengthen your rapport and the wellbeing of the client rather than representing a "breach of confidentiality".

4. A directive, proactive, and advocacy-oriented approach often is more effective than engaging in a lot of emotional reflection and open-ended discussions. South Asian clients often respond better to therapy when the clinician takes the lead rather than asking the client to reflect and take the lead. South Asian clients do not find much value in such a process, as they believe the therapist is the authority figure and knows best.

5. Integrating and applying culture specific anecdotes, proverbs, and lessons learned from mythologies and cultural folk tales can enhance the effectiveness of therapeutic engagement and understanding.

Zia: Major Depression in a Male Experiencing Domestic Abuse

Case History

Zia, a 63-year-old married Muslim male born and raised in India now living in the United States (U.S.), presented to an outpatient psychiatric clinic for treatment of depressive symptoms in the setting of marital discord and frequent non-compliance.

Zia immigrated to the U.S. in his early 20s. His birth and early development were unremarkable. His childhood medical history was significant for a mild traumatic brain injury, although other details of the injury are not available. He was a low average student. After high school graduation, he enrolled in a technical school but did not finish.

The same year he left school, his father died and his mother and older brother convinced him to get married. The matchmakers found him a proposal from a woman who was moving to the U.S. as she was sponsored by her sister. The families of both sides agreed to this marriage. He and his wife-to-be had little say in this marital arrangement.

Marital problems started almost immediately after marriage as both he and his wife considered their marriage a "duty" towards their families and accepted an "arranged marriage". They moved to the U.S. shortly after the marriage. They lived in different states with different family members and could not establish an independent livelihood as neither had a steady job. Zia could only find entry-level jobs that did not pay well. His wife constantly mocked him in front of her siblings and family members for not being as successful as them. Despite this, over the years they had two children. Frequent arguments and verbal fights were often triggered by poor finances. As the children grew older, they too did not respect their father as he was constantly taunted by his wife as a "poor provider."

Zia first came to psychiatric care as an inpatient in his late 30s after a non-life threatening gunshot injury that happened at work. Although he sustained a minor physical injury, he was emotionally distraught. At the time of the initial evaluation, he also reported several years of frequent bouts of prolonged, persistent depression with feelings of low self-worth, hopelessness, and suicidal thoughts. He denied suicidal intent or plan. He had never made a suicide attempt. Other symptoms included lack of joy and interest in life, poor sleep, constant worries, anxiety, fatigue, poor concentration, decreased appetite, and social withdrawal. There were no signs / symptoms suggestive of post-traumatic stress disorder, mania, or psychosis. There was no history of alcohol or substance abuse. His medical history was non-contributory. He had never sought psychiatric treatment in the past and there was no known family history of psychiatric illness. He reported marital discord and family conflicts leading to verbal abuse, belittling, and constant taunting by his wife as his major stressors.

His wife confirmed the lack of compatibility, but did not wish to do anything for fear of rejection by her family and community. She viewed his illness as a character problem. Although she felt cheated in life for not having a responsible husband who could provide for her family, she did not see divorce as an option since in her culture it would bring shame to the family.

Zia was diagnosed with Major Depressive Disorder and treated appropriately with pharmacotherapy. At the time of discharge, he was advised to have regular outpatient psychiatric care. However, he was non-compliant and stopped taking his medications. He remained stable for a short period but soon relapsed, which led to another hospitalization secondary to the severity of his depressive symptoms. Over the next few years, Zia was hospitalized about seven times. All his admissions were for severe depressive symptoms with suicidal thoughts, and all admissions were triggered by fights within his family

Outpatient psychiatric treatment continued between hospitalizations, but was not consistent. With outpatient treatment, Zia was gradually able to identify precipitating triggers. During the course of treatment, he also admitted to physical abuse by his wife and on one occasion even his adult son. His wife and children chose not to participate in his treatment, and his wife contacted the psychiatrist only when disability paperwork had to be done. In addition, he was made fun of by his family for having a mental illness and being in therapy, which largely contributed to the non-compliance.

Zia was eventually able to find a therapist that he connected with and saw more consistently. With the help of this therapist, Zia gradually reconciled to the fact that unless changes happened in his marital life, mood stability would be difficult. He began to see the dysfunction in his nuclear family and finally decided to move out of the house and to a different area, which led to discontinuation of treatment.

Diagnostic Formulation

Zia presented with classic symptoms of Major Depressive Disorder. Establishing a diagnosis of major depression was not a challenge in this case, but identifying the psychosocial stressors contributing to and maintaining his illness was a challenge, as Zia was not forthcoming and the family was not cooperative. Zia had several vulnerabilities that would predispose to the development of a mood disorder: low average performance in school, loss of father during teenage years, accepting family pressure to get married to a person of their choice, the stress of migration, and lack of employable skills. A major stressor, however, was the absence of a loving and supportive life partner with chronic verbal and physical abuse by his wife. Even though Zia had recurrent bouts of depression, he did not seek treatment until the gunshot episode that brought him to the hospital.

Management

At first Zia was reluctant to continue treatment, but gradually came around. The family, however, did not accept or participate in the treatment. This is not uncommon in the South Asian community as having a mental illness is considered a shame and embarrassment to the family. Patients and family often hesitate to seek treatment. South Asians are often unable to accept mental illness as bona fide medical illness. If one does get depressed, the expectation is to pull oneself up by the boot straps, go to work, and fulfill the assigned family role. The traditional Indian society is patriarchal. Men are expected to be the main breadwinners and work to support the family. Keeping feelings to oneself and not expressing to others is not uncommon. Zia broke all the rules of a traditional South Asian male by not being a breadwinner, not having a steady job, struggling with a mental illness, and obtaining professional help. The stigma of divorce, and subsequent family shame, was culturally unacceptable to Zia's wife and she chose to stay in the marriage despite their incompatibility. Divorce is considered a taboo in the South Asian culture and more so in his Muslim community. Muslim women have the right to divorce, but it is often considered evil and reprehensible. In cases of domestic strife, South Asians tend to draw children and other family members into the arguments, usually as an ally to the stronger of the two partners as seen in this case. Therapy helped Zia to take a bold step and move out of the house. Unfortunately, he moved to a distant place and was lost to treatment.

Zia's treatment included predominantly pharmacotherapy. Even though Zia was interested in family psychotherapy, his wife and children did not participate. They considered these sessions as "time away from work." They were, however, not against Zia taking medications, which they found less stigmatizing. Clinicians need to understand individual family dynamics and try to strike a balance between keeping the patient in treatment and engaging family members appropriately. However, no matter how hard the clinician tries, engagement of all family members may not be successful.

Summary

Zia is a 63-year-old married Muslin male of Indian descent who intermittently engaged in psychiatric care for treatment of Major Depressive Disorder in the setting of marital discord. This report illustrates the challenges in treatment of a South Asian male with long-standing depression, confounded by unhappy wedlock, financial problems, and a cultural stigma against family psychotherapy

Teaching Points

1. Domestic abuse can occur to males too. Clinicians should be aware of signs of abuse. Some of them include belittling, humiliation, name-calling, hitting, and controlling finances.
2. South Asian men are raised to be stoic and not express their emotions. It may take several sessions before patients or family members are comfortable enough to discuss their feelings and situations that trigger negative feelings. Clinicians need to be patient and give patients / families space and time.
3. If the family is not on board, clinicians need to be prepared to work with the patient without the family, to help strengthen coping skills.

Shaila and Harish: A Couple's Journey from Disparate Upbringing to a Family Unit

Case History

This case involves a married couple. The treating counselor received a call from the wife, Shaila, requesting an appointment for marriage counseling. She did not say much over the phone except that she and her husband were having difficulty in their marriage. Both Shaila and her husband, Harish, presented to the initial evaluation at the scheduled appointment time.

Shaila, a 38-year-old female, was born and raised in India. No perinatal problems were reported. Birth and developmental milestones were normal. She reported a happy childhood. Shaila was the oldest of three siblings and had a good relationship with her parents and siblings. Her parents lived in a mid-sized city in Southern India and were well off and well known in the community.

Growing up, most of the time, Shaila felt like her parents were there for her and she could be herself. Her love for reading was admired and fostered. She did very well in school and received top grades. Most things came easily to her. If something did not, she felt anxious and gave up easily. Shaila's experience of her mother was that she (mother) was a good person and was gracious. She also thought that her mother sacrificed too much for others, did not stand up for herself, and was too obedient. As for her father, she saw him as courageous, loving, and motivated. Her experience with her father was that he was short-tempered, critical, and domineering.

Overall, Shaila felt loved and cherished as a child. She looked up to her father and thought that her mother was weak. Shaila's parents followed Indian holidays but were not very religious.

As children, Shaila and her sister (two years younger) had many disagreements and arguments. Shaila was serious, stayed away from conflicts, concentrated on her studies, and received all the accolades while her sister was mischievous and often got into trouble with their parents for misbehaving. After Shaila moved to the United States (U.S.), she and her sister became closer and they talked often over the phone. As for her brother, there was a four year age difference and Shaila never felt close with him and never had much disagreements or arguments with him.

Shaila's parents had a good reputation in the society and had many good friends. A few relatives (e.g., uncles, aunts, cousins) lived near them. Shaila usually kept quiet, liked spending time by herself, did not get involved in gossiping, and had a decent relationship with her extended family members.

Harish, a 38-year-old male, was born and raised in India. He reported that he was the product of a healthy pregnancy and childbirth and that he experienced normal developmental stages. Harish and his parents lived in a small, rural area, where most people knew each other and had many relatives nearby. He came from a financially stable, but not rich or highly educated, family. His parents were traditional and religious people. His mother was a homemaker and his father provided for the family financially. Harish was the middle child with older and younger sisters. According to Harish, the siblings loved each other, but he did not feel closely connected. Harish said that his parents showed their love for him by showering him with special treatments that his sisters did not receive. He did not have to help with household work as his sisters did. He was expected to study and uphold the family name and make his family proud. He was held to very high standards and was yelled at and spanked by his father if he did not do what was expected of him.

According to Harish, he mostly felt lonely and did not feel listened to or understood most of his childhood. The praises he received for his academic achievements felt hollow to him. Harish's experience of his mother was that she was loving, caring, and giving. He also thought that she was anxious and too submissive and weak. She cried to him when she was stressed or unhappy and he comforted her by listening and talking to her, which made her feel better. His father was active, intelligent, and short tempered. Harish thought that his parents cared more about how they came across in the society than about their children. Harish mostly concentrated on his studies and did well academically.

Shaila and Harish fell in love during their college years. Harish admired Shaila's intellect, strong will, and her independent and vivacious personality. Shaila admired Harish's brilliant mind and what she perceived as a sophisticated and quiet self. They both pursued the Information Technology field, were married, and moved to the U.S. for work. Harish's mother was not happy about Harish's choice of his wife. She wanted to find a woman of similar psychosocial background for her son as other women of her age had done. She also did not care for Shaila's academic and professional achievements. She expressed that a woman's priority should be taking care of her husband and his family. According to her, Shaila was not taking care of Harish because she was interested in being a career woman.

Shaila had a shock of cultures the first time she visited Harish's family. She experienced the interactions of Harish's family as rude and unsophisticated. After their marriage, before they moved to the U.S., they lived with his parents for a couple of months as was culturally expected. During the above period, there was a lot of tension between Shaila and her mother-in-law. They had many disagreements and arguments. Shaila felt that even though she was equally educated to Harish, she was treated as inferior to Harish. She experienced her mother-in-law's behavior as overbearing, controlling, and manipulative.

Shaila felt that Harish cared more about his mother than her. She thought he sided with his mother whenever there were disagreements. It was painful to Shaila that her husband did not stand up for her. She felt alone without being able to feel safe emotionally with her husband. On the other hand, Harish felt stuck between the two women and felt bad for his mother since he was moving to the U.S., away from his parents. He could not understand why his wife was making a big deal about an elderly woman's (mother) opinions. As for her father-in-law, Shaila thought that he was too quiet, did not have a backbone, and let his wife do whatever she wanted.

After moving to U.S., Harish and Shaila both were looking forward to the new beginning. There were some adjustments to the new life, but they both immersed themselves into their work. The excitement of a new life, a passionate sex life, and having children carried them through the early part of their life in the U.S. However, every time they visited India or Harish's parents visited the U.S., all the problems intensified between the in-laws. Whenever they talked with or about Harish's mother, some issue came up that made the rupture in their relationship deeper and wider. Shaila felt that Harish's mother was trying to establish control over their life even from afar. There were tears, guilt tripping, and questioning from his mother at times. As a duty-bound Indian son, Harish felt guilty for being away and not taking care of his parents. Shaila's anger towards her mother-in-law only made it worse. After some time, Shaila stopped interacting with his family altogether, and he stopped talking or sharing information with her about his family. However, the tension continued. Both had started to walk on eggshells around each other not feeling safe to bring up any information about his parents. As for Harish's siblings, Harish and Shaila had no problems interacting with them, but they were not very close and there was not much interaction.

Over time, other issues cropped up in Harish and Shaila's marriage. He started to see Shaila's independent and strong willed personality that he had admired previously as stubborn, selfish, and angry. She started to see him as weak, nagging, irritating, and relentless. When she felt overwhelmed, she yelled and screamed or exited the room. Harish and Shaila both treasured their sons, ages six and three. They wanted to do the best for their children. Arguing in front of the children made them sad, but they did not know how to manage the situation. As for Shaila's family, Harish got along well with them and he respected them, especially her father. Her parents tried to help them by giving some advice, but that went nowhere. Overtime, Shaila and Harish started to sleep in different bedrooms and did not know how to reconnect. That is when they realized that they needed help and called a counselor.

By the time Shaila and Harish decided to receive counseling, they had a deep rupture in their marriage. They knew that they loved each other, but their defensiveness came to the forefront quickly. They had difficulty communicating appropriately. The pain of thinking that her husband did not care about her bothered Shaila a great deal. Every interaction was fraught with defensiveness, sarcasm, putdowns, and name calling. Neither one felt listened to or supported. Shaila's exiting when she felt overwhelmed with emotions only made it worse for Harish, who wanted to resolve things then and there. The passionate and loving periods had decreased over the years as the negativity and arguments increased. Even though they tried to keep the children out of it, there were times when they spoke through their children to one another. Both were stressed out and thought that the partner was ready to call it quits at any given moment.

Diagnostic Formulation

There was no evidence in this case for a diagnosis of major mental illness outside of the life story events. Even though Shaila and Harish were born and raised in India, they came from different family backgrounds. Shaila was raised in an affluent family and Harish a middle class family. Shaila experienced love and freedom. Her coping with issues was mostly by withdrawing and stuffing her anger. When anger intensified inside, she either exited from the scene or had an outburst. Harish, even though his parents praised his achievements, was yelled at if he did not get high grades in school. He coped with issues mostly by trying to do better at whatever he did. Harish's mother cried in front of him when she was unhappy in life. He did not like his mother crying. When she did, his way of coping was to make her feel better by talking to her.

As in most Indian families, Harish and Shaila's parents concentrated on their children's education. Harish and Shaila both focused on their education as well. They both thought that their mothers were weak. Shaila saw her mother-in-law as nagging, controlling, and relentless. Initially, Harish and Shaila were attracted to each other's energy and personalities, but over time, those traits started to become problems. When they disagreed, Shaila usually withdrew and exited, and Harish usually pursued with explaining and discussing the issue at hand. His communication style was overwhelming for her and her exiting was anxiety causing for him. She started to see Harish as nagging, controlling, relentless, and weak. He started to see her as stubborn, angry, domineering, and selfish.

As happens in many Indian families, Shaila and her mother-in-law both were competing for Harish's attention and affection. Harish, being an obedient Indian son wanting to please his mother, felt guilty about moving to the U.S.. He never establishing appropriate boundaries around his mother's demands. He also had difficulty showing his wife that she, his life partner, was important and her wellbeing was a priority for him. Neither one felt safe with the other. Their defenses came up quickly and it was easier to point fingers and blame than look at their part in the relationship issues.

Management

During the first session, some basic information about the couple was gathered, including the number of years Harish and Shaila were together and married, number and age of children, current living situation, prior counseling experience, health issues, employment, and special interests. The boundaries of counseling and the counseling process were explained. The importance of using "I" statements, listening, validating, empathizing, and respecting vulnerabilities were discussed. They were encouraged to share their deepest feelings and thoughts. They were told to never use the information obtained during the sessions to hurt the partner later. The focus of therapy was not about who was right or wrong but about how to help the partner understand and fulfil the needs while learning strategies to self soothe and be there for the partner.

The couples' sessions were of ninety minutes each. The counselor met each of them alone for a session (50 minutes each) the week after the intake to learn more about sensitive issues. During the following sessions, Harish and Shaila sat facing each other.

Initially, the counselor mirrored, validated, and empathized with each of them as they spoke since they had difficulty validating and empathizing with each other. After a couple of sessions, they were able to dialogue using the techniques with the counselor's assistance. They were able to reminisce about the time they fell in love and the happy memories of their relationship. At times during the sessions, both Shaila and Harish expressed their pain and anger. At times, they blamed each other for things that went wrong. The counselor helped them to communicate what they perceived and experienced.

Culturally, many mothers-in-law expect their daughters-in-law to be subservient. Shaila's mother-in-law expected her to be obedient and dutiful to Harish and his family, especially to her. Harish had difficulty seeing the impact of his mother's behavior on Shaila. Shaila did not want to be submissive like her mother and had set herself apart from cultural norms. As an independent woman with ambition and professional capabilities, she was happy that Harish initially liked her that way, however, she felt an external influence from her mother-in-law. Harish often did not have a clue about why Shaila was angry. When there were major arguments, he could see his wife's side, but still supported his mother.

During the sessions, the counselor helped Harish and Shaila remember how it was for them when they were in the romantic phase of their relationship; their early romantic interactions, how they felt about each other, and how they held each other in their vision. Small positive steps they made every day were incorporated into their structured dialogues. They both wanted to interact with each other as equal partners with respect and love. As for upbringing of their children, they were mostly on the same page. They discussed and agreed to work on their differences away from their children so the children saw a united front and respect between their parents. They worked on various grounding techniques and self-soothing skills to cope with their stress and anxiety.

During the sessions, Shaila and Harish were helped to re-image each other as wounded instead of dangerous. Both became good at holding the partner with respect while listening, mirroring, summarizing, and empathizing. They started to accept responsibility for their contribution to the rupture in the relationship. As each one felt understood, they also understood the underlying sadness and pain beneath their defensiveness and anger. When reflecting upon their childhood experiences, they were able to see some parallels between the partner and the pain they had experienced growing up with their parents. They worked on various strategies to foster empathy, listening skills, and coping skills. As they felt safe with each other, they were able to let go of the defenses. Small but consistent positive changes started to happen. Instead of complaining, they started to make requests that the partner could fulfill. Over time they learned to manage their emotions by self-soothing and learned to stay and listen to the partner.

Eventually, as Shaila and Harish started to see the relationship as a source of happiness and satisfaction, they started to sleep in the same bedroom. They could see that their children were happier as the positive changes started to happen between the parents. They persevered and worked together whenever one of the partners reverted to the old ways. Over time, Shaila and Harish were able to establish better boundaries with their extended family and a clear nuclear family as husband and wife with their children. It was difficult initially for Harish's mother. Respecting hierarchy and elders was important to her and obedience of her son and daughter-in-law was her way of getting respect. Harish played a crucial role in helping his mother understand what he needed from her to have a happy life and understand that he still loved her. As she realized that she could not influence Harish and could not change his behavior from a distance, she slowly stopped meddling in their lives. After sometime she started to show more acceptance of Shaila and they started to have positive interactions.

In the beginning, the 90 minutes sessions were scheduled once every two weeks except for the few times when they needed to see the counselor earlier. Over time, the space between therapy sessions increased. Eventually Shaila and Harish did not need therapy. The last time the counselor checked, they hardly had any major conflict and were very happy.

Summary

Shaila and Harish are a 38-year-old female and male, respectively, of South Asian descent who entered into couples therapy. The counselor saw Harish and Shaila as a couple yearning for connection. They had experienced connection, rupture, and disconnection. They did not know how to heal and reconnect. The disconnection in their relationship was in some ways replicating the experiences of disconnection with their parents. As partners, they were repeating some of the positive and negative emotional experiences of childhood. The core communication skill was used to move Harish and Shaila to reconnect. A safe structure supported them to deal with past, present, and future issues and associated emotions.

Harish and Shaila came to couple's therapy with many deep wounds created in childhood and through their relationship. The extended family, especially Harish's mother, made the situation more complicated. Through their intense work during and after therapy, the power struggle and rupture started to feel less catastrophic. They were able to manage conflicts by responding to each other with respect. As the external reactions were calmed during the sessions, the underlying need of wanting to be loved, respected, and supported came through. Both of their needs to feel safe and free inside the relationship became apparent. Ultimately, Shaila and Harish were able to make a conscious effort to reconnect, recommit, heal, and reawaken excitement and passion for each other. All the hard work the couple did also benefited their children. Both Harish and Shaila consciously and actively worked on improving their parenting skills. The children had observed the struggles their parents had experienced and they were now able to witness their happy lives together again. Neither Shaila nor Harish had any major mental illness. As their relationship healed and they learned to communicate appropriately and calmly, they were able to give and receive what they needed from each other.

Teaching Points

1. South Asian couples in trouble often refrain from seeking professional help secondary to shame or fear of being blamed for the relationship problems. They may also be under the misconception that their culture does not support psychotherapy.
2. South Asian marriages are based more on commitment than love. Couples often hesitate to seek professional help secondary to concerns that therapists may recommend divorce. In this case, there was both commitment and love. Therapy focused on not who is right or wrong and not on severing contact with extended family, but on strategies to resolve conflicts and make adjustments in their relationship. The counselor provided structure and a safe place for both of them to express themselves and improve their communication style. Through therapy, Harish and Shaila developed better coping skills to manage their emotions and to understand and fulfil each other's needs the best they could.

Sanju: Not All Marriages are Meant to Be

Case History

Sanju, a 40-year-old married male of Indian descent, presented for outpatient management of anxiety in the setting of marital discord.

Sanju was born in India. He immigrated to the United States (U.S.) at the age of 25 for higher education. Just prior to the move, he had an arranged marriage. Soon after his move, he joined a Masters course in Business Administration and completed it in two years. He later found a corporate job in New York and his wife, Seema, got a job at a bank in the same place. The first few years of marriage were uneventful. They had two children, a daughter and son, who were two years apart. Both children were healthy with no medical issues. Seema left her job to become a stay-at-home mother. Gradually, Sanju noticed a change in Seema's mood and behavior. She was moody, angry, irritable, and blamed Sanju for most things that went wrong. They often argued over trivial issues and these arguments always ended with Sanju taking the blame and apologizing. Seema blamed him for her miserable life. Sanju enjoyed interacting with his parents (who lived in India) weekly via telephone or Skype calls. He encouraged his children and wife to be part of the calls and to share stories. Seema not only disliked this, but would be angry and accuse him of being overly dependent on his parents. Gradually, her interactions with his parents stopped. Seema invited her mother to visit the U.S. and help her with their children. This also did not go well, as there were constant arguments between the two. Sanju suggested couples counseling several times, but Seema refused.

As time went by, Sanju realized being in the house and interacting with Seema was making him very anxious. Sometimes he would have anxiety attacks associated with physical symptoms of chest discomfort, sweating, and palpitations. These were always triggered by Seema's anger and rage. He coped by not reacting to any of her accusations, which further angered her. He finally decided to seek psychiatric help to learn coping skills and improve their relationship.

Psychiatric evaluation revealed that Sanju's anxiety was predominantly related to his wife's behaviors. Being around Seema made him very anxious. Otherwise, he was doing well. He was productive at work and had no issues getting along with supervisors and coworkers. He had a small social circle and healthy relationships with friends and extended family members. He was physically healthy and not on any medications. He did not drink, smoke, or use illicit drugs. He exercised regularly. There was no family history or past personal history of psychiatric illness. A diagnosis of Unspecified Anxiety Disorder was made and counseling was started. Therapy included a combination of supportive, interpersonal, and modified cognitive-behavioral therapy. He was not started on any medications. Sanju was very compliant with his follow-up visits. He took notes during the sessions and always did the homework given.

As Sanju was very interested in couples therapy, the psychiatrist suggested meeting with Seema individually for a couple of sessions and then starting couples therapy. At her first appointment, Seema informed the psychiatrist that there was no reason for her to have psychiatric treatment or be in counseling. She denied all psychiatric symptoms. She described Sanju as apathetic and a weakling who needed psychiatric treatment, as he could not stand up for himself. She was bothered by his weekly calls with his parents and considered this a major problem and an intrusion. She was raised by a single strict mother as her parents divorced when she was very young. She strongly disliked her father for leaving them and had no contact with him since her parents' divorce. She had a distant relationship with her mother and preferred Sanju to do the same. She articulated that Sanju was spineless, like her father. She acknowledged being angry and abusive towards him, but denied abuse of her children. She refused continued individual or couples counseling. She was not interested in working on their relationship, as she believed that there was: 'no relationship; no marriage'. She wanted to end the marriage.

Sanju continued with individual therapy. Through the regular follow-up sessions with Sanju, it was apparent that Sanju was a good provider. He earned well and provided his family a good home in an upper-middle class community. His wife had complete access to his finances. He talked to his parents weekly with his children when Seema was away, as he believed it was important for his children to know their grandparents. Because of his cultural beliefs of marriage being sacred and permanent, he did not want to end the marriage. He focused on being a better person to please his wife and learning strategies to cope with her anger. However, he was also fearful of her outbursts and the impact it might have on their children. He requested guidance from the psychiatrist on strategies to protect his children, should the situation become dangerous. The psychiatrist suggested calling the police. Two weeks later, Seema was in the kitchen cutting vegetables and arguing with Sanju. As the argument escalated, she threw a knife. This terrified Sanju and the children; he immediately called the police. By the time the police arrived, Seema had calmed down. She explained to them that it was a family dispute and an accident and convinced them it would not happen again. The police left after giving her a warning. No charges were filed.

As time progressed, Sanju and Seema drifted further apart. They began to sleep in separate rooms and have meals independently. Their interaction was limited to her requests for divorce and complaints about their children, as they seemed moody and their grades were declining. Sanju gradually lost interest in saving his marriage. He noted that his wife had already called it quits and was not interested in building their relationship or obtaining professional help. However, he was ambivalent about divorce secondary to cultural implications. Being a Hindu by birth, he maintained that marriage is sacred and permanent and that divorce might not be acceptable to his family and community. He also seemed unsure about the steps necessary for filing for divorce. He requested guidance from the psychiatrist.

Several sessions were spent on discussing his cultural values and the Hindu philosophy of marriage and divorce. Sanju learned that while marriage in Hinduism is considered sacred / permanent, there are circumstances in which the rule might have to be broken for the health and wellbeing of the couple or family. He also realized that a 'sacred relationship' can be re-interpreted as being responsible, accommodative, flexible, fulfilling the other's needs, and performing deeds where good outweighs the bad. The psychiatrist highlighted mythological stories of wars being fought for the good of humankind. Through these sessions, Sanju realized that his marriage had ended a long time ago and that granting divorce would be the responsible thing to do.

At Sanju's request, the psychiatrist suggested that he talk to a lawyer and open his own bank account as he had all his assets in joint accounts. The psychiatrist also suggested that he meet with his childrens' school guidance counselor and explain the family situation so that they could get much-needed help. Sanju carried out each of these suggestions. He felt less trapped. He began to speak up when he felt Seema's anger was baseless or directed towards the children. He met with a lawyer. He bought an apartment close to his house and moved out. He met with his children on the weekends. The children seemed happier and reported that their mother's anger outbursts were now under control. Finally, the divorce came through and Seema was happy with the alimony. Sanju's symptoms of anxiety gradually resolved. He was happy with the outcome and continued to work and maintain regular contact with his children.

Diagnostic Formulation

Sanju was diagnosed with Unspecified Anxiety Disorder. His anxiety revolved predominantly around his wife and their marriage. A diagnosis of chronic adjustment disorder would have also been appropriate. There were no other symptoms suggestive of major mental illness. Sanju was in an unhappy marriage; he and his wife were incompatible. Sanju tried to improve the compatibility by not reacting to his wife's anger; however, this only hurt him and the relationship. He was reluctant to end his marriage as he considered the union sacred and divorce culturally unacceptable.

Sanju sought professional help at the appropriate time to learn healthy ways of coping and adjusting. He was also interested in couple's therapy, but his wife chose not to participate. He continued individual therapy, participated actively, earnestly took notes, and completed the homework given at each session. He sought advice from his psychiatrist regarding problems he was unsure of and diligently followed her suggestions.

Through therapy, he was able to broaden his cultural perspectives and reframe values and beliefs contextually, both of which helped him make important decisions.

The reasons for Seema's anger and negativity towards Sanju is unknown. However, from the limited history, one may hypothesize that Sanju reminded her of her father, who she resented.

Management

The psychiatrist identified Sanju's desire to keep his family intact, protect his own integrity, and protect his children. Based on this, the psychiatrist suggested individual therapy for Sanju and couples therapy. However, his wife was totally against couples therapy as she was not interested in working on the relationship. Therefore, treatment was geared towards helping Sanju achieve healthy coping skills and problem solve using a combination of culturally flavored supportive, inter-personal, and modified cognitive behavior therapies. Medication was not initiated, as there was no indication.

Allowing Sanju to freely and safely express his feelings while developing self-awareness, healthy coping strategies, and appropriate interpretations of cultural values were the prime treatment strategies. Although Sanju saw himself as a punching bag for his wife, he also recognized that it was not a healthy way to cope. He gradually came to accept that his marriage was not salvageable and ending it was culturally appropriate. His priority shifted towards preserving his own integrity and raising healthy children.

Summary

Sanju is a 40-year-old married male of Indian descent who was diagnosed with Unspecified Anxiety Disorder in the setting of marital discord. He was constantly on the receiving end of his wife's anger. He sought professional help to learn coping skills to improve his relationship and save his marriage as it was important for him personally and culturally. However, through therapy, he learned to contextually reinterpret cultural values and take appropriate steps to maintain his health and the wellbeing of his children. His symptoms improved after divorce from his wife.

Teaching Points

1. Clinicians will encounter patients who require active guidance and direct recommendations for their problems. In this case, per Sanju's request, the psychiatrist had to outline the initial necessary steps for filing divorce (e.g., open own bank account, consult a lawyer, meet with the schoolteachers and guidance counselor, and call the police if situation is dangerous).
2. Clinicians must be able to educate and reframe cultural perspectives as simple practical solutions when patients tend to hold on to them rigidly and interpret them concretely.
3. Clinicians may help a patient reinterpret cultural values and take appropriate steps for own wellbeing and safety and the safety of his children.

Jaya: Cognitive Impairment in a Middle-Aged South Asian Woman

Case History

Jaya, a 66-year-old widowed female of Indian origin, was brought to an outpatient psychiatric clinic by her daughter-in-law for worsening behavioral issues. The family had recently moved from a different state in the United States (U.S.) because of the patient's son's work and were looking to establish medical and psychiatric care locally. Even though the psychiatrist, who was also of Indian origin, was fluent in the language spoken by this family, the patient spoke with a heavy regional accent, and it was difficult to obtain much information from her. Most of the history was obtained from the daughter-in-law.

The presenting complaint included a several-day history of sadness, anxiety, crying, and increased pacing, especially in the evenings. In addition, there were instances of urinary and occasional bowel, incontinence. She required assistance with some of her personal activities of daily living (ADLs), such as bathing, dressing, and toileting. She could feed herself. She was unable to perform any of the instrumental ADLs (IADLs), such as cooking, cleaning, shopping, and laundry. Her inability to independently take care of herself and perform IADLs was a change from her baseline, which had gradually declined in the last few years. She had never learned to drive nor manage bills and finances.

Her medical history was significant for hypertension, hyperlipidemia, and hypothyroidism. Pertinent negative history included acute cardiac syndrome, cerebrovascular accidents, seizures, and head trauma. There was no personal history of alcohol or other substance abuse. There was also no relevant family history of psychiatric illness, developmental disorders, or neurodegenerative disorders. At the time of outpatient presentation, she was on a mood stabilizer and an antipsychotic.

Collateral information was elicited from the patient's daughter-in-law (in-person), son (over the phone), and patient's sister-in-law (over the phone). It was learned that the patient had dropped out of school around 8th grade, whereas it was customary for females to complete at least a 12th grade education in the part of India she hailed from. She was considered cognitively slow by her family, but no medical evaluation was done to determine the cause. She was married by age 16, and the sister-in-law recalled that the patient struggled with household chores. She needed a lot of instruction and support from other adult females in the joint family household. She had three sons, but the middle son died around age five of an unknown cause.

Jaya immigrated to the United States with her husband, two young sons, and several extended family members in her early-30s. Her sons lived in close proximity, such that she continued to receive additional support with IADLs. Overall, she was doing well until about 9 years ago, with help from husband and extended family, except for occasional bouts of crying and bereavement over the loss of her son. She never received counseling or any type of mental health treatment.

Circumstances changed when her husband died suddenly of a stroke 9 years ago, and she lost her main support. Over the next couple of years, other family members of her generation also began to move away, as their respective children grew up and sought work elsewhere. Family members noted a gradual decline in her cognitive and functional capacity. She required assistance with tasks that she was previously doing independently. In addition, there was a significant change in her mood and behavior, with intermittent outbursts of verbal agitation (e.g. yelling, screaming), inconsolable crying, poor appetite, talking to self or unseen others, and insomnia. These outbursts led to three psychiatric hospitalizations over a span of 4-5 years, each about 1.5 years apart. She was treated with multiple psychotropics and given various diagnoses, such as schizophrenia, schizoaffective disorder, and bipolar disorder.

After discharge from the third hospitalization, she went to live with her second son and daughter-in-law. As time went by, the daughter-in-law, her primary caregiver, found it increasingly difficult to care for Jaya. She required assistance with her personal care and 24/7 supervision, secondary to her behavioral disturbances – agitation, crying, pacing, sleeping poorly.

Mental status exam at the time of the initial evaluation in the outpatient setting revealed an elderly South Asian female who appeared much older than her stated age. She was alert, not oriented to time or place (other than noting she was in the U.S.), but could tell her name and her daughter-in-law's name. There were no dysmorphic features. She was dressed appropriately and her hygiene and grooming were good. She appeared anxious and mildly psychomotor agitated. She did not speak English, but even her native language was noted to have word finding difficulties. Her speech content was poor, but thoughts organized and goal-directed. There was no evidence of formal thought disorder. She described her mood as "anxious" and her affect was constricted and appropriate to her mood. Her self-attitude was intact and vital sense poor. She seemed uncertain about the future. She denied suicidal or violent thoughts. At the time of evaluation, no delusions or hallucinations wwere observed (though daughter-in-law reported history of self-talk).

On cognitive exam, she was unable to state the date / day / month or name / address of the building. She could register three items, but could neither recall nor retrieve them with cues or recognize them. She was able to name a few simple items, such as pencil and watch, but not more complex ones, such as the lead of the pencil or dial of the watch. She was unable to copy the intersecting pentagons. She could not read or write in English. She could read a simple sentence in her native language, but not write a grammatically correct sentence.

Work up done in the outpatient setting revealed results of all blood work to be in the normal range. Magnetic resonance imaging of the brain revealed global atrophy.

Diagnostic Formulation

Based on the presenting history, collateral information, and work up, a diagnosis of Development Disorder of unknown etiology, mild degree of intellectual impairment / borderline intellectual functioning was made. Given the history of cognitive and functional decline from baseline functioning in the presence of clear sensorium, a diagnosis of Major Neurocognitive Disorder, probable Alzheimer's disease with behavioral disturbance, was also given.

Despite mild intellectual impairment and significant life stressors, such as the loss of a child and immigration, Jaya was able to function reasonably well secondary to adequate and consistent family support. This is not uncommon in the South Asian culture where family members live together or close by and help each other out. The traditional family structure used to comprise of a joint family, where adult sons, and subsequently their wives and children, continued to live with their parents. Thus, there could be multiple nuclear family equivalents within a joint family household. Such a family structure had the inherent advantage of having a large support system residing together, making it easier to care for one another in times of sickness, or through pregnancy and childbirth, and came with built in childcare support too. It also made it possible to provide long time or even lifelong support to those family members with chronic medical or mental health issues and intellectual disabilities. Not everyone was expected to succeed or excel at things. Awareness and access to healthcare, especially mental health care, was limited, and was accompanied by stigma and fear of prejudice. Hence, Jaya's limitations remained a fairly well guarded family secret.

The loss of her support system correlated with worsening in her condition. At times, this was severe enough to necessitate inpatient psychiatric hospitalization. It remains unclear whether the patient truly had manic or psychotic episodes leading to the diagnoses she was initially given. The unfamiliar setting of an inpatient psychiatric unit, and the absence of a person accustomed to her way of speaking, could have been additional barriers in arriving at a more accurate diagnosis. Other possible differential diagnoses could be major depression along with bereavement, as well as behavioral issues resulting from her intellectual disability and major neurocognitive disorder. It is to be noted that open expression of grief is culturally more acceptable in India, and stoicism is not expected, especially from women. Professional mourners or moirologists are also common in some Indian subcultures and are called *Rudaali*. Thus, Jaya's episodes of crying could have potentially been her way of expressing grief over the loss of her son, and later, her husband.

Management

The differential diagnosis was discussed with the daughter-in-law and she was encouraged to have the patient's son also come along for future visits. They were offered appointment times such that this would be possible. The family, which did not fit in the "model minority" stereotype of Indian immigrants, was not well versed with medical and especially mental health, issues.

The family was provided with extensive psychoeducation and encouraged to ask questions. Initially some medication changes were made to address the worsening agitation with good results. However, the patient's cognitive decline continued and she deteriorated further over the next year or so and became progressively harder to care for at home.

It was only at this point that the option of in-home care versus placement in a dementia care facility was brought up, keeping in mind the possible impact this suggestion would have on the son and daughter-in-law. They were provided with ample time to process this option and were reminded to not think of this as a reflection on their love or concern for their mother. They were encouraged to involve relevant family member in the decision-making process.

Had the patient continued to live in a large household as she did when she was in India, it would have been easier to care for her at home, with caregiving responsibilities being jointly born by various family members, thus reducing caregiver burnout. This was also compatible with the cultural value of revering ones' elders and caring for them in their old age. Even though the family structure in India has undergone radical transformation, from a joint family to a three-generation / nuclear family, values and expectations have not kept up with that pace of change. This is important to remember when treating patients who might need long-term placement.

In the joint family structure of a patriarchal society such as India, the eldest male is considered the head of the family, and the younger family members often seek his counsel in important matters. The eldest female tends to wield considerable influence on the daughters-in-law and is often the repository of culture and traditional values followed in the household. With such an exalted status within the family, when such elders become ill or decline with age, they continue to be respected and cared for, even at a personal cost to the children. Placing them in a facility would be considered a sign of disrespect and often frowned upon by society.

Jaya's son reached out to his younger brother, and to other elders in the family, and gained their support to place the patient in a nursing facility. As noted before, several of the older family members, who had emigrated from India, had passed away. The ones that remained were either born or had grown up in the U.S., thus their personal values aligned more closely with Western values. No other family members were able to care for Jaya around the clock, given her degree of cognitive impairment. Thus, with much deliberation and support, they were able to overcome the guilt and stigma related to placement.

Summary

Jaya is a 66-year-old widowed female of Indian origin who had a lifelong developmental disorder of unknown etiology with mild intellectual impairment and developed a progressive neurodegenerative disorder (likely Alzheimer's disease) later in life. She immigrated to the U.S. with her extended family in her early 30s. Because of strong support from close and extended family members, she was able to function reasonably well until her mid-fifties, when the support system gradually collapsed. Subsequent to the loss of that structure, death of her husband, and her own cognitive decline, she began to display behavioral disturbances that were initially addressed conservatively. These symptoms eventually required her to be placed in a nursing facility, a step that was quite difficult for her family to take because it was not in keeping with their cultural values.

Teaching Points

1. It is important to understand developmental and age appropriate functioning in a cultural context, especially in older immigrants, in order to assess for cognitive decline.
2. Given the largely collectivistic attributes of the Indian diaspora, sick or impaired elders tend to be treated with more tolerance and affection.
3. Suggesting moving a loved one to an assisted living facility or nursing home may elicit feelings of shame, guilt, and fear of criticism in family members. Such conversations need to be handled with a lot of sensitivity and support.
4. Many older immigrants from India tend to be less fluent in English and this might make it harder for them to avail of social activities and other services provided at senior centers. This may increase reliance on in-home care, increasing the financial burden of caring for such adults with cognitive impairment.
5. There are pockets of regions within a foreign country where immigrants from a particular subculture may live in close proximity, providing familiarity, comfort, and support to the expatriates. The burden of immigration may not be fully experienced by such people until they move out of this comfort zone, and this is important to factor into clinical decision-making.

Printed in the United States
By Bookmasters